Acting Edition

The Incomparable LouLou

A Comedy by
Ron Clark

Based on a Play by
Pierre Barillet
and Jean Pierre Gredy

Copyright © 2002 by Augustus Productions, Inc.
All Rights Reserved

THE INCOMPARABLE LOULOU is fully protected under the copyright laws of the United States of America, the British Commonwealth, including Canada, and all member countries of the Berne Convention for the Protection of Literary and Artistic Works, the Universal Copyright Convention, and/or the World Trade Organization conforming to the Agreement on Trade Related Aspects of Intellectual Property Rights. All rights, including professional and amateur stage productions, recitation, lecturing, public reading, motion picture, radio broadcasting, television, online/digital production, and the rights of translation into foreign languages are strictly reserved.

ISBN 978-0-573-62875-7

www.concordtheatricals.com
www.concordtheatricals.co.uk

FOR PRODUCTION INQUIRIES

UNITED STATES AND CANADA
info@concordtheatricals.com
1-866-979-0447

UNITED KINGDOM AND EUROPE
licensing@concordtheatricals.co.uk
020-7054-7298

Each title is subject to availability from Concord Theatricals Corp., depending upon country of performance. Please be aware that *THE INCOMPARABLE LOULOU* may not be licensed by Concord Theatricals Corp. in your territory. Professional and amateur producers should contact the nearest Concord Theatricals Corp. office or licensing partner to verify availability.

CAUTION: Professional and amateur producers are hereby warned that *THE INCOMPARABLE LOULOU* is subject to a licensing fee. The purchase, renting, lending or use of this book does not constitute a license to perform this title(s), which license must be obtained from Concord Theatricals Corp. prior to any performance. Performance of this title(s) without a license is a violation of federal law and may subject the producer and/or presenter of such performances to civil penalties. Both amateurs and professionals considering a production are strongly advised to apply to the appropriate agent before starting rehearsals, advertising, or booking a theatre. A licensing fee must be paid whether the title(s) is presented for charity or gain and whether or not admission is charged. Professional/Stock licensing fees are quoted upon application to Concord Theatricals Corp.

This work is published by Samuel French, an imprint of Concord Theatricals Corp.

No one shall make any changes in this title(s) for the purpose of production. No part of this book may be reproduced, stored in a retrieval system, scanned, uploaded, or transmitted in any form, by any means, now known or yet to be invented, including mechanical, electronic, digital, photocopying, recording, videotaping, or otherwise, without the prior written permission of the publisher. No one shall share this title(s), or any part of this title(s), through any social media or file hosting websites.

For all inquiries regarding motion picture, television, online/digital and other media rights, please contact Concord Theatricals Corp.

MUSIC AND THIRD-PARTY MATERIALS USE NOTE

Licensees are solely responsible for obtaining formal written permission from copyright owners to use copyrighted music and/or other copyrighted third-party materials (e.g. artworks, logos) in the performance of this play and are strongly cautioned to do so. If no such permission is obtained by the licensee, then the licensee must use only original music and materials that the licensee owns and controls. Licensees are solely responsible and liable for clearances of all third-party copyrighted materials, including without limitation music, and shall indemnify the copyright owners of the play(s) and their licensing agent, Concord Theatricals Corp., against any costs, expenses, losses and liabilities arising from the use of such copyrighted third-party materials by licensees. For music, please contact the appropriate music licensing authority in your territory for the rights to any incidental music.

IMPORTANT BILLING AND CREDIT REQUIREMENTS

If you have obtained performance rights to this title, please refer to your licensing agreement for important billing and credit requirements.

ROYAL POINCIANA PLAYHOUSE
OPENING NIGHT
JANUARY 21, 1986

THE ZEV BUFMAN THEATRE PARTNERSHIP, LTD
Zev Bufman, Lawrence Kasha & David Landay

present

LINE RENAUD
in
THE INCOMPARABLE LOULOU

A Comedy By
RON CLARK

Based on a Play by
PIERRE BARILLET and JEAN PIERRE GREDY

with

BARBARA CASON	LISA FELCOSKI	JOHN FIELDER
STAN FREEMAN	KENNETH MARTINEZ	ROBERT PINE

Scenery By
PATRICK HUGHES & CHRISTOPHER MANDICH

Costumes By
NOEL TAYLOR

Lighting By
JAMES RILEY

General Management
THEATRE NOW, INC.

Production Stage Manager
MICHAEL J. FRANK

Music
LOULOU GASTE

Directed By
CHARLES NELSON REILLY

CHARACTERS

Benji	STAN FREEMAN
LouLou	LINE RENAUD
Harold Bowman	JOHN FIEDLER
Candi	LISA FELCOSKI
Barbara Milner	BARBARA CASON
Peter Desmond	KENNETH MARTINEZ
Jack Latham	ROBERT PINE

THE SETTING
The Action takes place in LouLou's Manhattan apartment in the West Forties

THE TIME
The mid 80s

ACT I

Scene 1

LATE AFTERNOON
(As the curtain rises, we see BENJI [BEN] FIRESTONE. LOULOU's accompanist and friend, put the finishing touches on an arrangement at the piano. He's wearing a tuxedo with the jacket off.
The high-ceilinged apartment is located in a renovated manufacturing building, situated on the West side of Manhattan, not far from the Hudson River.
Through the large manufacturers' type of windows, we see a similar building across the street, as well as a number of New York skyscrapers in the distance.
The apartment consists mostly of a very large room with wood floors. A mirrored wall spans the entire 4th wall facing the audience. The apartment is sparsely decorated. There are pieces of furniture here and there, such as sofas, chairs, coffee tables, several half empty cardboard boxes, an open sidewalk cafe umbrellas, and an antique grandfather clock, near the front door. The baby grand piano is Stage Left, down from the front door. On the wall, next to the piano, are bookshelves with some books and some record albums. There are several large, framed posters of LOULOU on the walls. The posters are at least twenty years old; a few are from the Casino de Paris Revue and feature LOULOU in a seductive pose. One is from Las Vegas, with the words "The Incomparable LouLou" printed across it. There are also several very large black-and-white photographs of LOULOU taken with various famous people, such as Bob Hope, Charles De Gaulle, Ed Sullivan, Maurice Chevalier, etc.

THE INCOMPARABLE LOULOU

Upstage, facing the windows, We see a section of the kitchen. We can see part of an industrial-size stove, the kind used by short-order cooks. Also partly visible is a very large restaurant-type freezer.

There is one piece of furniture in the apartment that seems very much out of place. It is a writing desk, possibly dating back to the Louis XVI period, know in France as an écritoire. It should be apparent that this apartment has only recently been moved into.

Downstage Right are several steps that lead to platform and corridor which leads to O.S. bedroom. LOULOU's posters and pictures also adorn these walls.

BENJI is very cynical. He rarely smiles. He speaks to LOULOU, O.S.

LOULOU speaks English with a thick French accent.

The action takes place in the early 1980's.)

BENJI. *(Calls out.)* I'm all set, LouLou. Let's rehearse it, okay?

LOULOU. *(O.S., shouting.)* Okay, okay. Don't rush me!

BENJI. Save your voice for tonight. So the emcee says, "And now, ladies and gentlemen, the beautiful Boom Boom Room, in downtown Staten Island, is proud to present that mischievous mademoiselle from Montmartre. That singing sensation from the River Seine. The one, the only, the Incomparable LouLou!" *(LOULOU enters, in casual attire, carrying a makeup case and a boa.)* Applause, applause, applause. And the band goes ...*(BENJI plays intro music as LOULOU deposits makeup case near piano and wraps boa around her neck.)* One, two, three, lights, five, six, and ...

(LOULOU examines herself in mirrored wall [4th wall] and turns to BENJI.)

LOULOU. Stop! *(He stops playing.)* You did not tell me how you like my new mirror wall.

BENJI. Terrific. Now you don't have to turn around to see the factory across the street.

THE INCOMPARABLE LOULOU

LOULOU. *(Proudly.)* Today a factory—Tomorrow a "condo-minimum."

BENJI. *(Checks watch.)* LouLou, we have a show to do in exactly three hours and fifty-four minutes.

LOULOU. Okay. Okay.

(LOULOU continues to check herself in the "mirrored wall".)

BENJI. *(Assuming the role of the emcee again as he plays fanfare.)* So ... Direct from the Ed Sullivan Show ...

LOULOU. He's been dead for years.

BENJI. The star of the Casino de Paris ...

LOULOU. Nobody cares.

BENJI. And of that hit recording, "La Vie Est Belle ..."

LOULOU. Who remembers?

BENJI. That little package from Paris, France ...

LOULOU. *(Looking at herself in "mirror".)* Not so little anymore.

BENJI. A great big Staten Island welcome for the one, the only, the Incomparable LouLou ... *(BENJI plays intro again as LOULOU takes flashlight from top of piano and uses it as microphone.)* One, two, three, lights, five six, and—

LOULOU. *(Singing.)*
HELLO, WE MEET AGAIN
 BENJI. Diction.
 LOULOU.
YOU LOOK AS WONDERFUL
AS YOU DID THEN
 BENJI. We're in America.
 LOULOU.
MY HEART IS FILLED WITH HAPPINESS
AND I AM THRILLED WITH WORDS I CAN'T EXPRESS

(Addressing imaginary audience.) Allo, Staten! My favorite island in the world. You came. You saw, Your remembered. *(Reacts to imaginary response.)* What do you mean, you don't remember? *(Turns*

to BENJI.) See? I told you they would not remember. Maybe I try something more *sophistiqué*. What if I come out and the stage is dark, and I stand here like this, with my back to the audience?

(LOULOU demonstrates, stands with her back to the audience.)

    BENJI. *(Sarcastically.)* That's clever.
    LOULOU. Then a spotlight hits me on the head ... *(She demonstrates the spotlight hitting back of her head.)* You play a little something background ... *(BENJI starts playing appropriate background music.)* Bon. Then I turn slowly, like this, and I act surprised. *(She turns, jumps back, as if surprised by "audience".)* Oh! You scare me. Merci, merci, mille fois, merci. Comme ça fait longtemps qu'on s'ait vue. Je suis tellement heureuse d'être parmi vous à cette occasion la plus merveilleuse ... In other words ... *(Waves.)* "Hi!" *(BENJI has stopped playing. She looks over at him.)* Too *sophistiqué*?
    BENJI. Not if you take out that French stuff. Let's do it the way we rehearsed it, okay?

(BENJI plays. LOULOU begins to sing.)

    LOULOU.
HELLO, WE MEET AGAIN ...

(HAROLD BAINS, a smallish, middle-aged caterer, enters, carrying trays of food, a bouquet of flowers, and a bottle of champagne. He and LOULOU acknowledge each other in the mirrored wall. He makes several trips to hallway, dancing to the music, as LOULOU continues singing. HAROLD is also wearing a tuxedo.)

    LOULOU. (Cont.)
YOU LOOK AS WONDERFUL
AS YOU DID THEN
MY HEART IS FILLED WITH HAPPINESS
AND I AM THRILLED WITH WORDS I CAN'T EXPRESS

THE INCOMPARABLE LOULOU

HELLO
WE NEVER MET
LET'S MAKE TONIGHT A NIGHT WE WON'T FORGET
I KNOW THAT SMILE
YOU BET I DO
AND WHERE'S THAT SEXY ONE
OH, HERE, IT'S YOU ...

(HAROLD does a few sexy steps to the music. LOULOU stops singing.) Harold, my dear, dear Harold.

(They exchange kisses on the cheeks. HAROLD offers food from one of his trays. LOULOU takes a piece of celery.)

HAROLD. Hi, Benji. How's the music business?
BENJI. *(Who has stopped playing.)* There is none. How's the catering business?
HAROLD. Fantastic! The leftovers *alone* can earn you a nice living. *(Suddenly realizing.)* Listen, if I'm interrupting anything ...
BENJI. *(Sarcastically.)* Of course not. We were just about to take five. That's how we do it. We work five, we take five ...
LOULOU. I'll go get my gown.

(LOULOU starts toward bedroom.)

HAROLD. *(Holding up bottle of champagne.)* I brought you champagne for the celebration after your show.
LOULOU. Thank you.

(LOULOU blows a kiss to HAROLD and exits.)

HAROLD. You'll be happy to hear I cleaned out the van. Yes sir, we're going in style tonight.

(HAROLD goes to phone and dials.)

BENJI. *(In a monotone.)* Whoopee!
HAROLD. *(Into phone.)* Bernice? Harold ... Harold Bains ... *Your husband.* *(Aside.)* What a sense of humor. *(Into phone.)* What do you mean the Meyers postponed the bar mitzvah for next week? *Nobody postpones a bar mitzvah* ... I don't care if they are reformed ... I don't know what time I'll be home, Bernice. It's and opening.

(HAROLD hangs up. Sighs. LOULOU re-enters from bedroom with a garment bag which she hangs up.)

LOULOU. How is Bernice?
HAROLD. You know Bernice. Bernice is Bernice.
BENJI. That's good to hear. Now, can we get back to our rehearsal? We've gotta leave in twenty minutes.
HAROLD. *(Referring to flowers he put on piano; to LOULOU.)* How do you like the flowers?
LOULOU. Beautiful. Another wedding?
HAROLD. No, a 65th anniversary. *(To BENJI.)* Can you imagine being married to the same person sixty-five years? *(BENJI shakes his head "no" while LOULOU nods "yes".)* No wonder they didn't want the flowers. *(Hands LOULOU very large container of ground coffee.)* Here's that new coffee I've been telling you about. Part caffeine—part decaffeinated. Gets you to bed at a reasonable hour. *(Offering food from a try.)* How about some cheese puffs? Or as you would say, cheese poofs.
LOULOU. You know, Harold, finding me this apartment was more than I could ever ask. You don't have to bring me food *every* day.

(LOULOU takes coffee to kitchen.)

HAROLD. Then how about a croissant to make you feel at home?
LOULOU. No, thank you.
HAROLD. Remember when she first came over here? Nobody knew what a croissant was. Now they're very popular.
LOULOU. Now they are, and I'm not.

THE INCOMPARABLE LOULOU 13

(HAROLD spots her antique piece of furniture near entrance to bedroom and goes to it.)

HAROLD. Hey, your écritory sure looks good in here.
LOULOU. *(Correcting him.)* Écritoire.
HAROLD. Whatever.

(LOULOU joins HAROLD next to the écritoire and strokes it gently.)

LOULOU. Mon trésor. My other best friend. *(To écritoire.)* Late at night, we still have our conversations. I'll bet it's worth a bundle by now.
LOULOU. It's my aces in the holes. It's what I save for the day it rains.
BENJI. Yeah, well, it's starting to drizzle. *(Plays musical vamp.)* And ...

(LOULOU sings the same opening number once more, only this time, in French.)

LOULOU.
JE VOIS PARTOUT
DES SOUVENIRS
AH QUE C'EST BON BON BON
DE REVENIR
DE VOIR VOS YEUX
VOTRE SOURIRE
OH LA LA LA
ÇA FAIT PLAISIR
CAR TOUS CEUX
QUE JE RETROUVE ICI
SON POUR MOI
COMME DE VRAIS AMIS

PARDONNEZ-MOI
DE M'ENTENDRE DIRE
C'EST TELLEMENT BON ...

Telephone rings. BENJI slams piano with both hands.)

BENJI. Ah, merde.

(LOULOU goes toward phone.)

LOULOU. I will hang up right away. *(She picks up phone.)* Allo?... *(Her expression changes.)* Who? *(Visibly shaken, as she sits down.)* Yes, quite a surprise ... *(BENJI and HAROLD begin to take notice.)* No, it's just that I never expected to hear from you after all these years... No, more like nine. As a matter of fact, almost ten. *(BENJI and HAROLD exchange knowing, concerned glances.)* Yes, I'm fine. Everything is fine ... I'm a little rushed, I'm on my way to a very important singing engagement ... *(She slowly turns her back to HAROLD and BENJI, who stand nearby.)* Tomorrow? You mean you're here in New York? ... Well, I don't know. I ... Could you hold on a minute? *(Covers phone; to HAROLD.)* Would you hang this up. I'll take it in the bedroom.

(LOULOU hands him the phone. He takes it, covers it.)

    HAROLD. It's him, right?
    LOULOU. *(As she heads for bedroom.)* Him?
    BENJI. Yes, him.
    LOULOU. Oh, him.
    HAROLD. *(Disgusted.)* Him.

(LOULOU exits to bedroom.)

    BENJI. *(Calls out.)* Make it short.

THE INCOMPARABLE LOULOU

(As soon as LOULOU's left, BENJI goes to HAROLD. HAROLD holds phone between them as they listen to conversation.)

LOULOU. (O.S.) *(Calls out.)* You can hang up now!

(HAROLD reluctantly hangs up phone. They sit on sofa during the following and nibble on some of HAROLD's food.)

HAROLD. What the hell does *he* want?

BENJI. How's that for timing? *(A beat.)* Did you know he was a congressman now?

HAROLD. Figures

BENJI. He and that woman he married are all over the social columns running to parties and dances and fund-raisers.

HAROLD. *(A beat.)* I wonder who's catering all those parties.

BENJI. This could affect her performance tonight.

HAROLD. She'll be all right. I'm more worried about the place you got her working in. Is it classy enough?

BENJI. It's the best I could do. Thank God, the owner remembered her hit record.

HAROLD. *(Insulted.)* Why wouldn't her remember "La Vie En Belle?" Everybody does.

BENJI. It's "La Vie *Est* Belle." "La Vie *En* Rose"—But "La Vie *Est* Belle." Get it?

HAROLD. So, that's still no reason why he shouldn't remember it.

BENJI. First of all, that song was over thirty years ago, and the owner's only twenty-six.

HAROLD. I sure hope this isn't going to turn out like her other comebacks.

BENJI. She didn't come back for her last two comebacks. At least she's here and she's doing it. *(Calls out.)* LouLou!

HAROLD. Is George coming?

BENJI. I don't think so. He's staying home. He's making another one of his soufflés. How much sugar can I eat? It's ridiculous for a man my age to break out. I have to get kids to go into drugstores to buy my Clearasil.

(LOULOU re-enters room.)

>LOULOU. Okay, let's continue.
>HAROLD. Him, right?
>LOULOU. Why is everybody so afraid to mention his name?
>BENJI. Who?
>LOULOU. Him. I mean, Jack. Okay, so now that we all know my ex-husband called, can we continue?
>HAROLD. You gonna see him?
>LOULOU. Tomorrow, for a drink ... dinner, maybe. He ran into my best friend in Paris, and she gave him a present for me. She also gave him my new number.
>BENJI. *(Annoyed.)* Why the hell did she have to do that?
>HAROLD. Do you think that's such a good idea to see him? I mean, after everything you went through? I mean ...
>LOULOU. I'm all better now, Harold. Don't worry. I'm also older.
>HAROLD. Age has nothing to do with this.
>BENJI. We just don't want you to get hurt, that's all.
>LOULOU. You two worry too much. Come on, let's rehearse. Let's do the waltz.
>BENJI. *(Returns to piano.)* All right, the waltz. I'll give you four.

(BENJI plays and counts off four bars of music.)

>HAROLD. By the way, Bernice said that if you sing tonight like you did at our wedding, you'll be great.

(HAROLD sits down, all ears.)

>LOULOU.
>EEF I LOVE ...
>>BENJI. *(Correcting her.)* If.

LOULOU.
IF I LOVE
IF I FALL IN LOVE
IT CAN'T BE
WITH JUST A PART OF ME
I MUST BE ALL IN LOVE

(Doorbell.)

BENJI. We're still rehearsing.

(LOULOU continues singing as she motions to HAROLD to stay put while she goes to door and opens it.)

LOULOU.
IF I CARE
IF I DARE
GIVE MY HEART TO YOU

(At the door is CANDI, a very young, very pretty girl, about nineteen years of age. She's holding some sheet music. CANDI is wearing an outrageous outfit made from bits and pieces of everything. But it somehow looks good on her. LOULOU, while singing, kisses her on both cheeks and indicates to her to come in. CANDI enters. She exchanges smiles with HAROLD. She checks her hair in the "mirrored wall" and then sits on one of the stools at the piano and watches LOULOU, taken with her voice and her talent.)

LOULOU. *(Continuing during the above.)*
IT WILL HAVE TO BE
MY DARLING
FOR MY WHOLE LIFE THROUGH

BENJI. Keep singing.

LOULOU.
SO I'M UNDER YOUR SPELL
HOW CAN I TELL
IF THIS IS MEANT TO BE TRUE

    BENJI. We go up a half key.
    LOULOU.
IF I LOVE
IF I LOVE ...
IF I FALL IN LOVE
I MUST FALL IN LOVE WITH SOMEONE
SOMEONE WHO IS SURE TO BE ...

    BENJI. Now, hold this next note.
    LOULOU.
ALL ...
    BENJI. Not forever.
    HAROLD. Great!
    LOULOU.
IN LOVE
WITH ME.

(BENJI stops playing. HAROLD and CANDI applaud enthusiastically.)

    BENJI. Okay, I give up. Who is she?
    LOULOU. She's my new best friend from downstairs, on the first floor.
    CANDI. My name is Candi, like in chocolate bar, but with an "i."
    LOULOU. Candi with an "i." *(To BENJI.)* You hear that?
    BENJI. No, I'm on a break.
    LOULOU. This is Ben Firestone. My musical director. Benji's been with me since I come to America.
    BENJI. I was just a kid then.
    CANDI. LouLou told me all about you. You live with a guy named

THE INCOMPARABLE LOULOU

George, and you fight a lot ... *(BENJI throws a look at LOULOU.)* My old man is a musician. He has a heavy metal band.

BENJI. *(Half groaning.)* Oh, my God.

CANDI. He lets me sing with them sometimes.

LOULOU. She's lucky he lets her do *anything.*

CANDI. He's not so bad, LouLou.

LOULOU. And this is my other best friend, Harold Bains.

HAROLD. *(Gets up, takes CANDI's hand and kisses it.)* Enchanté.

CANDI. Neat. *(Looks around room.)* Boy, this place is starting to look great.

LOULOU. *(Reaching for CANDI's music.)* I asked her to bring her music. She sings quite well. She writes all her own songs. Do you want to hear her?

BENJI. Why don't we hear the singers in the order in which they arrived?

LOULOU. *(To CANDI.)* He'll hear you some other time.

CANDI. Oh, sure. Of course, I'm nothing like LouLou. But then again, I don't speak French. I love everything French, don't you? French doors, French pastry, French kisses ... *(HAROLD and BENJI react.)* That's not an electric piano, is it?

BENJI. *(Becoming more annoyed.)* No, this is *not* an electric piano. I have *never* played an electric piano, I *will never* play an electric piano! My nightmare is to be sentenced to *die* in an electric piano!!!

CANDI. *(Innocently—to HAROLD.)* What's wrong with an electric piano?

HAROLD. *(Shrugs.)* Don't ask me. I'm a caterer.

BENJI. *(Calming down—smiles condescendingly.)* The *performer* is the one who should be electric, *not* the piano.

CANDI. Shhh ... *(She stops and listens. They all look at one another.)* Did anyone hear a puppy barking?

(CANDI goes to front door, opens it for a moment.)

LOULOU. What poupée?

CANDI. My old man just bought me the cutest little dog. He always buys me something when he's feeling guilty.

LOULOU. What did he do this time?

CANDI. Don't ask.

BENJI. Good. I won't ask either. Now can we get back to work?

(BENJI starts playing.)

CANDI. *(As she sits on the sofa.)* Absolutely. She has a show to do.

BENJI. *(As he plays her opening number.)* From the top. One last time.

LOULOU.
HELLO, WE MEET AGAIN ...
(She spots a straw hat on piano.)
I have an idea. Play it a little slower.
(Sings as Maurice Chevalier.)
HELLO, WE MEET AGAIN
YOU LOOK AS WONDERFUL
AS YOU DID THEN
MY HEART IS FILLED WITH HAPPINESS
AND I AM THRILLED WITH WORDS I CAN'T EXPRESS ...

(BENJI stops playing.)

LOULOU. Why you stop?

HAROLD. Yes, why you stop?

BENJI. If they wanted Maurice Chevalier, they would hire Maurice Chevalier.

LOULOU. Well, they would have a little trouble finding him these days. (BENJI gets up.) What are you doing?

BENJI. I'm getting up.

LOULOU. Why?

BENJI. I always get up before I start walking. I find it's easier on my legs. We better get going.

THE INCOMPARABLE LOULOU

LOULOU. *(Suddenly nervous.)* Benji, cancel the engagement.
BENJI. What are you talking about?
LOULOU. I can't do it. I'm too nervous.
BENJI. LouLou, don't start. It's been too long since your *last* job. You don't want the public to forget you. Besides, you don't cancel like that at the last minute.
HAROLD. *(Meekly.)* He's right. Even nightclub owners have feelings.
LOULOU. What if my comeback does not work?
BENJI. I don't believe this.
LOULOU. I have a knot right here in the pits of my stomach. I can't even breathe. *(She demonstrates by over exaggerating her inability to breathe.)* I am having a spasm.

(Once again, she demonstrates by acting out a series of spasms that are more like comic convulsions.)

CANDI. That's good. That means you're on edge.
LOULOU. I have gone *over* the edge. I forget all the words.
BENJI. *Hum.* They won't know the difference. It's Staten Island.
LOULOU. I'm so scared. It's like starting from scratching. I have no style.
BENJI. Your style is to sing the actual notes. It'll be very refreshing to people.
LOULOU. Benji. I want you to call the owner of the club and tell him I lost my voice .. or maybe I break a leg. No, make it two legs.
CANDI. But you've worked so hard these last few days.
HAROLD. Days! How about years?
BENJI. Okay, I wasn't going to tell you this.
LOULOU. *(Suspiciously.)* What?
BENJI. You're not going to like hearing this.
LOULOU. *(Growing impatient.)* What?
BENJI. I better not tell you.
LOULOU. What? What?
BENJI. Okay. Do you have any idea how hard I had to work to get

the owner of the Boom Boom Room to hire you?
LOULOU. (A beat while it sinks in; then, infuriated.) What?!
BENJI. (To others.) See? I shouldn't have told her.
LOULOU. You had to talk a little pipsqueak on the tiny Island of Staten into hiring a big, international star like me?
BENJI. Well, it's just that ...
LOULOU. Me, who, in my first year in America, worked fifty-one weeks and six days straight ... I took off a Monday to get married. Me, who set a record in Las Vegas for the most consecutive performances by a human ... The Marquis Chimps still hold the record for animals. Me, who worked through stomach aches, back aches, pneumonia, laryngitis, arthritis ... (With determination.) Benji! Start playing! We'll show him what big-name entertainment is.

(Everybody's suddenly smiling again. BENJI resumes playing.)

HAROLD. (Caught up in the excitement.) No wonder, there's no business like it.
LOULOU. (With more enthusiasm than ever.)
DO YOU LOVE ME
JE VOUS AIMES BEAUCOUP
LET ME SHOW IT
WITH A KISS FOR YOU

I WANT TO SAY
HOW NICE YOU ARE
BONSOIR, BONSOIR
BONSOIR, MY FRIENDS
BONSOIR

I'll get the dress.

(They all applaud. LOULOU grabs her garment bag. Everybody swings into action.)

THE INCOMPARABLE LOULOU

BENJI. (Grabbing mujsic off piano.) I got the music.
CANDI. I got the albums.

(She reaches for the cardboard box.)

HAROLD. I got the food. (Reaching for bags of food.) Wait till you see what I packed for us tonight.
BENJI. We're not going on a cross-country trip, Harold. We're going over the Verazzano Bridge.

(BENJI puts his tuxedo jacket on.)

HAROLD. So what? A person's gotta eat.
LOULOU. Are you sure I need to bring my records?
HAROLD. Absolutely. I guarantee you'll sell plenty after the show. (With apprehension.) Is your sister coming?
BENJI. Does Dracula stay home at night?
LOULOU. Barbara will meet us at the club.
CANDI. (Opens the front door.) I've got your makeup case. And don't take the elevator. Yesterday it got stuck.
BENJI. How could you tell?

(CANDI, HAROLD, and BENJI go off singing La Marseillaise. *LOULOU turns off the light switch at the door, turns and addresses the écritoire which is still bathed in a bit of light.)*

LOULOU. Bonsoir, mon trésor. Wish me luck. If all goes well tonight, I'll buy you that lamp I told you about.
BENJI. (O.S.) LouLou!

*(LOULOU closes the door and exits.
Blackout.)*

Scene 2

(It is later that night. We hear the sound of keys, followed by the door opening. HAROLD enters first. He turns the lights on. He's carrying the makeup case. He puts it down near the sofa and pours two stiff drinks. He holds one out at arm's length.
A moment later, BENJI enters, arm stretched out. He immediately goes for the drink. They take a long sip, sigh, then sit.
CANDI enters, carrying boa, garment bag, and box of record albums.)

CANDI. (Crossing to bedroom. In a half whisper.) Personally, all I think she needs is a new act. A new look, new pictures, new clothing, new arrangements—(To BENJI.)—no offense.

(CANDI goes into the bedroom.)

BENJI. New arrangements. Believe me, this was a much better business when Madonna was in church instead of record stores.

(LOULOU enters, wearing her gown, equally dejected.)

HAROLD. Where should I put your makeup?
LOULOU. Take it home to Bernice. I'll never use it again. (She reaches for BENJI's drink.) Give me that, Benji.

(LOULOU sits on sofa.)

BENJI. You don't like scotch.
LOULOU. I know.

THE INCOMPARABLE LOULOU

(BENJI goes to bar and pours himself another glass of scotch. CANDI re-enters from bedroom.)

CANDI. *(Walking over to the bottle of champagne.)* Doesn't anybody want champagne?
LOULOU. Most people don't drink champagne at a funeral.
HAROLD. It's that damn comic that went on before you. He ruined it for you. What a sleaze.
LOULOU. *(Who has taken a sip of the scotch, makes a face.)* This tastes terrible.
BENJI. *(Going to retrieve her glass.)* Here, I'll change it for you.
LOULOU. No, this is what I deserve.
HAROLD. How the hell do you follow a man who bills himself as "The dirtiest mouth in New York"?
BENJI. You never should've let him talk you into using some of his jokes.
LOULOU. *(Suddenly realizing.)* Hey, where's my sister?
BENJI. Who cares?
LOULOU. I thought she was following us.
CANDI. Maybe you shouldn't have done any French songs.

(CANDI pours a few glasses of champagne.)

HAROLD. What's the difference? They didn't understand English either. It was the wrong crowd.
LOULOU. I don't think you can use the word crowd for six people.
BENJI. When I told the owner how bad the piano was, he couldn't believe it. He said he just had it painted.
HAROLD. And the nerve of that guy, to force me to hang around for a second show, knowing full well there wasn't going to *be* a second show.
BENJI. He's a kid, what do you expect?
HAROLD. He didn't even have a sign out front.
CANDI. He did so have a sign. It said "Budweiser".

BENJI. I'm telling you, this whole business is getting so young, it's disgusting. Last week I had a meeting with a new agent—I swear, the kid was thirteen, tops. I think his father bought him the agency for Christmas. I spent the first twenty minutes trying to explain who Cole Porter was. He thought it was some sort of ale.

HAROLD. You can't hate a guy just for being young.

BENJI. *(Quickly.)* Yes, you can. I never wanted to be young. Even when I was young I *hated* being young. I hate everything young, including Loretta and Robert.

CANDI. *(Confused.)* Who are Loretta and Robert?

(All three slowly look at CANDI.)

HAROLD. Did you notice the lighting.

LOULOU. *(Finally deciding to speak up.)* It's no use crying over the milk that is spoiled. My type of singing does not exist anymore. There are no more clubs for me, there are no more records, and there is no more TV. The sooner we all realize that, the better off we will all be.

(Sound of impatient doorbell.)

CANDI. *(Goes to door.)* Maybe it's my old man. I left a note downstairs.

LOULOU. That can only be Barbara.

(CANDI opens the door—standing there is a rather elegant woman with a heavy tan, wearing a tailored black suit and hat, holding a Doubleday bookstore shopping bag. She's dressed expensively. She is LOULOU's half-sister, BARBARA. She is American and has no French accent whatsoever.)

BARBARA. *(As she enters—talking past CANDI to LOULOU.)* Do you realize I lost part of my tan riding in your goddamn elevator! I timed it. Fourteen minutes to get to the fifth floor.

CANDI. We didn't meet. I'm LouLou's neighbor from downstairs.

LOULOU. That's Candi with one "i". My sister, Barbara. *(Proudly.)* Candi makes all her own clothes.

BARBARA. *(Mock surprise.)* No kidding.

CANDI. I hardly hear your French accent at all.

BARBARA. *(Dryly.)* That's probably because I don't have one. Our father traveled a lot. He went everywhere. How he missed Staten Island I'll never know. And besides, we had totally different mothers.

LOULOU. She loves to say that.

BARBARA. We're half-sisters.

(BARBARA picks up a glass of champagne.)

BENJI. Which disproves the theory that half a sister is better than none.

BARBARA. *(Looks at BENJI; sarcastically.)* Cute. *(Notices mirrored wall and recoils.)* Oh, my God, this wall is all mirror. For a moment I thought you had two of these places. *(Sips champagne. To HAROLD.)* Nice champagne. What month?

HAROLD. *(Indicating the apartment; proudly.)* So, how do you like LouLou's new apartment?

BARBARA. You know, I think I once saw an off off-Broadway play in this place. *(A beat.)* That didn't work, either. *(To LOULOU.)* Do you realize, you're practically at the corner of Twelfth Avenue? *(LOULOU is about to answer.) Nobody* lives near Twelfth Avenue. I didn't even know this city went past Ninth.

LOULOU. *(Finally able to get a word in.)* But that's why I have such a beautiful view of the River Hudson.

BARBARA. *(Going towards windows in kitchen area.)* What view?

LOULOU. You have to lean out.

BENJI and HAROLD. *(In unison.) Way* out.

BARBARA. *(Looking out window.)* I still don't see the river.

CANDI. You will, as soon as they tear down that building across the street.

BARBARA. *(Incredulously.)* *Why* would they tear down *that* building before this one?

HAROLD. *(Proudly—pointing.)* That's New Jersey over there.

BARBARA. Is there no end to this apartment?

LOULOU *(As she gets up and heads for bedroom.)* Benji, would you fix me another terrible scotch, while I go change?

BENJI. *(Goes to bar.)* Sure.

CANDI. Shhh ... *(She listens as others stay quiet.)* Do you hear any barking?

BARBARA. I don't think the little animals in this building do that.

CANDI. *(Goes over to LOULOU.)* Thanks again for letting me come tonight. I just *love* hearing you sing.

LOULOU. Thank you, Candi.

CANDI. Bye, y'all!

(CANDI exits.)

HAROLD and BENJI. *(Both depressed.)* 'Bye.

LOULOU. *(To BARBARA.)* You want to see my bedroom?

BARBARA. *(Following LOULOU, with mock innocence.)* Is the industrial motif carried throughout the apartment?

(BARBARA and LOULOU exit to bedroom.)

HAROLD. You know, his calling before the show didn't help matters.

BENJI. I hate that man so much.

HAROLD. What are we gonna do, Benji?

BENJI. What do you mean, what are *we* gonna do? You'll go back to your fun-filled catering business and I'll go back to those wonderful singing auditions that I love so much.

HAROLD. I never realized till tonight, when I was watching her

sing, how much I depend on her. The joy she brings me.
BENJI. But you're a happily married man.
HAROLD. I'm talking about joy, not marriage. That woman has ... pizzazz. I don't know what else to call it. All I know is that when she's working, I feel alive. I feel like I'm part of it. *(A beat.)* Why can't things be like they used to be?
BENJI. You're a dreamer, Harold.
HAROLD. And you're not?
BENJI. I don't have dreams. I have nightmares—like the thought of having to go back to that piano bar where I used to work, accompanying a lot of lonely old ladies who sing off key. Answering requests like, "Play 'Sometimes I Wonder'".
HAROLD. What's "Sometimes I Wonder"?
BENJI. What they mean is ... *(Sings to "Stardust Melody")*
SOMETIMES I WONDER
WHY I SPEND THESE LONELY NIGHTS ...
HAROLD. *(Imploringly.)* You'll find her more work, won't you?
BENJI. *(After a beat.)* Where?
HAROLD. There's got to be something. *(Reaching into his jacket pocket.)* Look what I did to celebrate her opening. I named a sandwich after her. *(He pulls out a folded menu.)* I was going to show it to her tonight, but I don't think she's in the mood for food right now. *(He unfolds the menu and shows it to BENJI.)* There it is, the "Incomparable LouLou" sandwich. *(As he reads off the menu:)* It's twelve feet long. It'll serve up to fifty. It's got pastrami, salami, chopped liver, baloney, your choice of corned beef or roast beef. Pickles, Swiss cheese, tomatoes, mayonnaise, lettuce, sauerkraut, a thin layer of avocado, some Russian dressing and, of course, it comes on French bread.
BENJI. It's an incomparable sandwich, all right. I'm sick just hearing about it. *(He discards menu on sofa. Sound of phone Ringing. They look at each other. It continues to ring during the following.)* Who the hell calls at this time of night?
HAROLD. Drunks and perverts.

(HAROLD and BENJI walk to phone and stand there.)

BENJI. *(Looks towards bedroom.)* She isn't picking it up.

HAROLD. You wan to answer it?

BENJI. Maybe it's the kid who owns the club. Maybe he wants his money back. Go ahead, answer it.

HAROLD. *You* answer it.

BENJI. Why should I?

HAROLD. Okay, I'll answer it. *(He picks up the phone; into phone)* Yes? ... (Immediately covers mouth piece.) It's him. *(Into phone in a Chinese accent.)* I'm afraid you have wrong number ... *(As self.)* How did you know it was me? And how do you know I'm not at someone else's house? ... *(Cups phone again.)* He wants to speak to LouLou.

BENJI. Tell him she's sleeping.

HAROLD. Then what are *we* doing here?

BENJI. *(Going to piano.)* I got it. Tell him she's too busy to come to the phone. She's got a wild party going and the place is mobbed.

(BENJI starts playing loud, party-type music.)

HAROLD. *(Into phone.)* I'm sorry. I can hardly hear you. The place is packed with people celebrating LouLou's opening tonight. I'm afraid you'll have to call back.

(HAROLD slams phone down as BENJI abruptly stops playing.)

BENJI. We've got to keep that man away from her.

(BENJI gets up.)

HAROLD. How do we do that?

(LOULOU re-enters room, wearing a robe, followed by BARBARA.)

LOULOU. What was all that noise?
BENJI. What noise?

THE INCOMPARABLE LOULOU

LOULOU. And who called?

(BENJI looks at HAROLD.)

BENJI. Uhh ... George. He just finished a crême brulée. He wants me to come right home and taste it.

(HAROLD goes to LOULOU, puts his arms on her shoulders.)

HAROLD. There was nothing wrong with you tonight, LouLou, that a "live" audience couldn't fix..
LOULOU. You're a good friend, Harold. Merci. *(She kisses HAROLD on both cheeks.)* I'm sorry about your van.

(LOULOU kisses him on both cheeks.)

HAROLD. Hey, what's a couple of broken headlights! I look at it this way: You go to Staten Island, you pay a price. I'll call you tomorrow. *(He goes to the door—to BARBARA.)* Goodnight, Wicked Witch of Scarsdale.

(BENJI and LOULOU smile. BARBARA gives him a condescending look. HAROLD exits.)

BENJI. Sleep in tomorrow.

(BENJI goes to LOULOU.)

LOULOU. Thank you for everything, Benji. I'm a very lucky woman to have friends like you and Harold ... *(She kisses BENJI on both cheeks.)* My love to George.
BENJI. By the way, he wants to have you over for dinner some night next week. He's got a new Mandarin chocolate soufflé he's dying to try on you. I swear, it's like being married to Fanny Farmer.
LOULOU. As soon as I lose one pound, I'll be there.

BENJI. *(At the door—to BARBARA.)* That was wrong of Harold to call you the Wicked Witch of Scarsdale ... You don't live in Scarsdale any more.

(BENJI exits, closes door.)

BARBARA. Is he becoming less gay or am I becoming more tolerant?
LOULOU. Let me put it this way. You will never be as tolerant as he is gay. *(BARBARA lights a cigarette.)* So, tell me about your honeymoon.
BARBARA. *(Sits down and removes her shoes.)* Don't remind me. We went to Grenada in the Caribbean. Remember that island we attacked? Believe me, it wasn't worth it. There isn't a decent hotel on the entire island. And you should see the way they make martinis. They put salt on the rim.

(BARBARA makes a face.)

LOULOU. Well, how was this honeymoon compared to the others?
BARBARA. You've seen one, you've seen 'em all.

(BARBARA extinguishes her cigarette.)

LOULOU. My sister, the romantic.
BARBARA. Yeah ... *(Indicates apartment.)* Look where it got you. *(Reaches into her purse and takes out a letter.)* Well, now that we've put your career to rest, you might be interested in this letter that was waiting for me when I got back.

(BARBARA hands letter to LOULOU, who starts reading it. BARBARA walks around, behind sofa.)

LOULOU. *(Confused.)* I don't understand.

THE INCOMPARABLE LOULOU 33

BARBARA. What's to understand? Doubleday is interested in publishing your memoirs. They're drawing up the contract.

LOULOU. But how did they get them? *Why* did they get them? *You* were not even supposed to see them. I only gave them to Melissa because she said she wanted to know more about her favorite aunt.

BARBARA. Well, now she does. And so do I. And so does Doubleday. *(She reaches for shopping bag and starts retrieving books from it.)* Look at these. Shelley Winters, Lauren Bacall, The ever-popular Joan Collins. And let's not forget Shirley MacLaine. *(She deposits four more books.)* She's not even that old and she's already milked her life with four of these. Now, if they can do it, why can't you?

LOULOU. *(Gets up.)* Because my memoirs are *my* memoirs. They are not for the publique. I only wrote those things because it was part of my therapy. Do you forger?

BARBARA. *(Knowingly.)* Who can forget a major breakdown?

LOULOU. *(Defensively.)* It was an average, normal, everyday breakdown.

BARBARA. There was nothing average, believe me. You went catatonic when Jack left you.

LOULOU. Don't exaggerate.

BARBARA. Then who caused you to go into that depression that kept you from working all these years?

LOULOU. I can't help it if my style went away.

BARBARA. It's not your style that went away, Louise. It's *you* that went away. You disappeared for an entire year.

LOULOU. My doctor said I had to find myself.

BARBARA. Yeah, you found yourself. You found yourself without a husband and without a career.

LOULOU. *(Handing BARBARA her purse and shoes.)* I think you should leave now.

BARBARA. You know, you wouldn't be in this mess had you married that orthodontist I introduced you to years ago.

LOULOU. I did not like him.

BARBARA. I thought he was terrific.

LOULOU. Yes, I know. That's why you married him.

BARBARA. Well, he was terrific ... for awhile. And what was wrong with the chiropractor?

LOULOU. Maybe you're just better at picking husbands because you do it so often.

BARBARA. At least I don't crumble when they leave me. I take the settlement and I go on to bigger and better things. I've earned it, I get it. I use it. God, I've never heard of anyone not taking alimony from an ex. You're in trouble, Louise. *Big* trouble.

LOULOU. I've been in big trouble before. And stop calling me Louise. My name is LouLou.

BARBARA. Don't you see what's going on here, *LouLou*. You're broke. You are living in a factory. You've practically sold everything you ever owned.

LOULOU. *(Offhandedly.)* I gave most of it away.

BARBARA. You know, the trouble with giving to those less fortunate than yourself is that one day you wind up being the less fortunate one.

LOULOU. I am rich in other ways. I have wonderful friends.

BARBARA. You mean that bunch of parasites.

LOULOU. Parasites? I am the one who takes from them.

BARBARA. Have you forgotten what you've given them? You made Benji your musical director, you gave him a place to hang out, a reason to live. You put Harold into the catering business. Your friends have done very well for themselves.

LOULOU. And what about you? You forgot what I did for *your* career.

BARBARA. What?

LOULOU. I put you in business. I paid for your first wedding dress.

BARBARA. Cute.

LOULOU. Anyway, I forbid you to say another word about my friends.

BARBARA. Lou, grow up. Friends are not the answer right now. Right now what you need is "money." *(Holding up letter.)* And I happen to have found a way for you to get some.

THE INCOMPARABLE LOULOU

LOULOU. Do you really think America cares if I fool around twenty-five years ago with Charles Aznavour and Yves Montand ... Separately, of course.

BARBARA Don't you understand? It's your association with the Alain Delon, the Belmondos, the Truffaut.. That's what they're interested in.

LOULOU. But they're all French.

BARBARA. Excerpt for Congressman Latham.

LOULOU. Why would anyone be interested in my life with Jack?

BARBARA. Your ex is big news now. He has his picture all over the place. He's been twice on Donahue. Jack is becoming quite a celebrity. Interesting, isn't it? He's become what you were.

LOULOU. My private life with Jack is private. You don't do that to people. It's cheap. It's undignified. And I'm not going to do it.

BARBARA. You know, you're a damn fool, Lou. Here you are with one foot in the Hudson River while he and his grand lady are galavanting all over the world. Don't tell me you didn't see last month's *Cosmopolitan.*

LOULOU. *(Mock shock.)* Oh, my God, I missed it.

BARBARA. There's a wonderful article about how a young congressman from Arizona left an older French singer ten years ago to marry Senator Caldwell's daughter. Great picture of her ... *(Shows her profile.)* with her new nose.

LOULOU. Well, she needed one.

BARBARA. And you need this book—and we're going to publish it.

LOULOU. No, we're not. Now please go.

BARBARA. I'm telling you right now, I can only stall the publishers for so long.

LOULOU. So long.

BARBARA. *(Miffed.)* Well, you won't have to say *that* again.

(The following lines are delivered in quick succession.)

LOULOU. You promise?
BARBARA. *(Opens front door.)* We're through.
LOULOU. Good.
BARBARA. Good.
LOULOU. When will I see you again?
BARBARA. Monday—with the contract.

(They quickly kiss on the cheeks. BARBARA exits.)

LOULOU. *(Calls out.)* Don't take the elevat ... *(Dismisses it with hand gesture.)* Take it.

(LOULOU closes door. She goes to the sofa to lie down. She puffs up a few pillows. She suddenly notices HAROLD's menu. She starts reading it. A smile crosses her face as she reads off a few of the ingredients in her sandwich.)

LOULOU. (Cont.) "Salami, chopped liver, mayonnaise, sauerkraut, avocado ... " *(To écritoire.)* Life is so crazy. Just when you worry you may never eat again *(Holds up HAROLD's menu.)* ... you *become* a sandwich.

(Fast Fade Out.)

Scene 3

(The following day. Early evening. BENJI is at the piano, accompanying CANDI, who is singing a rock and roll song. BENJI is visibly pained as he bangs away at the simple chords. CANDI is wearing another wild outfit. The front door is open. PETER DESMOND, a young antique dealer, is busy writing out a check, which he leaves on the ´écritoire, There are several discarded dresses draped on the sofa, chairs, etc. The cardboard boxes have been removed.)

THE INCOMPARABLE LOULOU

CANDI.
IF YOU STEP ON MY FACE
WITH SPIKES ON YOUR SHOES ...

BENJI. *(Incredulous—as he looks over sheet music.)* If you step on my face with spikes on your shoes?

CANDI. Can't you play it more hip?

(She bangs out the beat in the faster rhythm. BENJI resumes playing as PETER goes to sofa, sits, sips his coffee, and continues to enjoy CANDI's performance.)

CANDI. (Cont.)
IF YOU STEP ON MY FACE WITH SPIKES IN YOUR SHOES,
IF SLAPPIN' ME SILLY KEEPS YOU AMUSED,
IF MY BODY ENDS UP LOOKING LIKE ONE BIG BRUISE ...

(To BENJI.)

"G."
I WON'T RUN FOR COVER

(To BENJI.)

"G-7."
BABY, YOU'RE MY LOVE
TELL ME I'M YOUR LOVER, TOO, AND I'LL RECOVER,
I'M YOUR LOVE SPECIMEN, I'M YOUR LOVE SPECIMEN ...

(CANDI starts laughing as LOULOU enters from bedroom, wearing a gaudy, outdated, '20s dress with lots of frills. BENJI sees her and immediately segues into Charleston music. LOULOU starts dancing and singing.)

LOULOU.
CHARLESTON, CHARLESTON
LA LA LA LA, LA LA ...

(She stops, looks at CANDI. BENJI stops playing.)

Too short?
CANDI. Too gaudy. You can't go out on a date wearing that.
LOULOU. Dress number nine coming up.

(She turns to go.)

PETER. *(Calls out.)* LouLou?
LOULOU. *(Stops.)* Yes?
PETER. I left your check on your écritoire.
LOULOU. Thank you, Peter. I will come by and have coffee with you next week.
PETER. Oh, you can come and visit your clock anytime. I'll repair the chimes and price it especially high so it'll be there in case you want it back some day.
LOULOU. Thank you.

(She exits to bedroom as PETER goes to CANDI.)

PETER. Nice meeting you both. I especially liked your lyrics.

(BENJI gives him a look.)

CANDI. Thanks. *(To BENJI.)* Maestro.

(PETER proceeds to take the antique clock out to hallway during the following.)

BENJI. Can we take a break now?

(BENJI gets up, goes to bar to refill his glass.)

CANDI. WE just took a break.
BENJI. You don't want to push a voice like yours too far.

(LOULOU re-appears at bedroom door. She's holding two dresses on hangers. Both old-fashioned and inappropriate. She holds one up high.)

LOULOU. Candi?
CANDI. No. *(LOULOU holds up the other.)* No. Don't you have anything in black?
LOULOU. *(A beat.)* I think I have the perfect dress.

(She quickly turns and exits.)

CANDI. I realize this is not your kind of music. Maybe that's why you're having so much trouble.
BENJI. Listen kid. I came here today out of the kindness of my heart.
CANDI. We both know why you came here today. To keep an eye on LouLou.

(PETER has left.)

BENJI. I'm helping you, aren't I? This kind of music is hard on my fingers ... not to mention my ears.
CANDI. I hate to be the one to tell you this. But musically, you're living in the past.
BENJI. *(Smiles broadly.)* Thank God.
CANDI. *(Indicating piano.)* Shall we? And try not to lose the tempo.

(BENJI, resigned, rolls his eyes and returns to piano. He begins playing the "clang, clang" background notes as CANDI goes to front

of piano and resumes singing;)

CANDI. (Cont.)
IF YOU CALL ME A PIG, I'LL ANSWER THE CALL,
'CAUSE, DADDY, YOU CAN MAKE ME SQUEAL AND SQUALL
JUST WRAP ME UP AND TAKE ME HOME AND HAVE A BALL.
YOU DON'T HAVE TO BASTE ME, BUT YOU MUSTN'T WASTE ME,
SPRINKLE ME WITH SUGAR AND C'MON AND TASTE ME.
YOU'RE MY LOVE SPECIMEN ...

(LOULOU re-appears once again, wearing yet another dress. This time she has on a very, very tight-fitting black dress. She can hardly move in it. She takes tiny steps as she walks forward. CANDI stops singing and bursts out laughing. BENJI stops playing.)

CANDI. (Cont.) Well, it's your basic black.
LOULOU. *(Looks at self in mirrored wall.)* See what happens when you have a caterer for a friend? I look like a sausage. Maybe I can do a T.V. commercial for Hebrew National.

(LOULOU laughs. CANDI quickly goes to her, gets down on her knees, next to LOULOU, and starts examining the sides and the hem of the dress.)

CANDI. At least it's not as gaudy as the others.
LOULOU. You know, this dress has seen more action than the New York Rangers.
CANDI. *(Excited.)* You like hockey?
LOULOU. Not, but I used to like action. *(Laughs. CANDI rips open one side of dress.)* What are you doing?
CANDI. We're in luck.
LOULOU. We are?

THE INCOMPARABLE LOULOU

(CANDI goes to other side and rips that one open as well.)

CANDI. I might be able to sew this up. Do you have any pins?
LOULOU. In the bedroom, next to the bed.

(CANDI quickly exits to bedroom.)

BENJI. *(Coming toward LOULOU, drink in hand.)* You're actually excited about this "date," aren't you?
LOULOU. When you go out with you ex-husband who is married, I don't think it's called a date.
BENJI. What would you call it?

(CANDI returns with small box of pins.)

CANDI. I'd call it thrilling. Are you going to go to bed with him?
LOULOU. *(Reprimandingly.)* Candi! *(BENJI shakes his head and sits. He keeps himself busy doing a crossword puzzle in newspaper.)* Well, he was your husband first.

(She starts pinning LOULOU's dress.)

LOULOU. You know, just because I'm French does not mean ... I'm French.
CANDI. Don't move.

(CANDI accidentally pricks LOULOU.)

LOULOU. OWW!
CANDI. You moved.
LOULOU. I moved because you made a hole in me.
CANDI. You never did tell me how you met your husband.
BENJI. *(Correcting her.)* Ex.
CANDI. Ex.
LOULOU. He was in Paris at a public relations convention. That's

what he used to do before he became my manager.)
CANDI. Then he saw your show and fell madly in love with you.
BENJI. Then he saw his meal ticket and brought her to America.
LOULOU. Benji!
CANDI. Did you and your *Ex* ever consider having children?
LOULOU. *(Reminiscing.)* I was going to take time off from work, but one job followed another, then another ... Remember how we never stopped, Benji? Anyway, finally, when I decided to have a baby, he decided to have a divorce. *(CANDI looks up at her, smiles sadly.)* I always dreamed of having a girl like you.

(She touches CANDI's hair softly.)

CANDI. *(Finding the moment a little awkward, then:)* When I get married, I don't think I'll see my ex-husband after I'm divorced.
LOULOU. Did you hear that, Benji? This is the way young people plan marriage today.
BENJI. Just listen to their music. *Nothing* will surprise you.
CANDI. *(Indicating side of dress.)* Do you want slits?
LOULOU. *(Looks at self in mirror.)* Non. Slits are for sluts.
CANDI. Sometimes I wonder if it was so smart of me to leave home and come here.
LOULOU. Where are you from?
CANDI. The Dakotas.
LOULOU. There's more than one?
CANDI. Yeah, two. I'm from a little town right on the border of North and South. You probably never heard of it. It's called Thunder Hawk.
LOULOU. And you probably never heard of my town. It's called Valence.
CANDI. How come "Valence" sounds so much better than "Thunder Hawk'?
LOULOU. Because the grass is always greener ... *(Reminiscing.)* in the south of France.

BENJI. While we're in France, girls, what's a six-letter word for a French border lake, beginning with A-N?
LOULOU. Annecy. A-N-N-E-C-Y.

(BENJI nods "thank you.")

CANDI. I'm surprised you didn't go back after ... you know ...
LOULOU. My career slowed down there, too. Besides, I don't have any more family back home. And my close friends are all here.

(LOULOU looks over at BENJI.)

CANDI. *(With a sudden perplexed look on her face—hesitantly.)* You're gonna hate me.
LOULOU. *(Confused.)* What do you mean?
CANDI. You're really gonna hate me.
BENJI. *(Growing impatient.)* Okay, so she'll hate you.
LOULOU. *(Fearing the worst.)* You don't sew.
CANDI. *(Cringing.)* I do. But I forgot about my old man hocking the sewing machine.
LOULOU. Hocking? Is that like hockey?
BENJI. *(Pleased.)* She doesn't have a sewing machine, so you won't be able to go. I'll tell Jack when he gets here.

(He gets up.)

LOULOU. Wait! You know, Candi, one of the best things about life is the unexpected. Because, with the unexpected you have to improvise. And when you improvise, some of the most creative ... *(Sound of knock on door.)* Oh, my God, it's him. *(Looks at herself in "mirrored wall".)* Looks like I will be wearing slits after all. Benji, get the door. Candi, get the dresses, get the pins.
CANDI. *(Gathering everything.)* You're wearing them.

44   THE INCOMPARABLE LOULOU

(LOULOU and CANDI quickly exit to bedroom as BENJI goes to door. Opens it. It's HAROLD. He's loaded down with balloons in all colors. Some are in the shape of clowns, others say, "HAPPY BIRTHDAY, STEVIE." He also has trays and boxes of food, including large containers of ice cream plus cookies, small sandwiches, and lemonade.)

BENJI. *(Calls out.)* It's only Harold!

HAROLD. Thank you. Quick, the ice cream is melting. *(BENJI helps him carry the food to the kitchen freezer.)* I think I saw him.

BENJI. *(Taking some of the items from him.)* Where?

HAROLD. Circling the block in a big black limo ... that you and I pay for with our tax dollars.

BENJI. *You* pay for. I'm not working that much these days.

HAROLD. I think I prefer a party of fall-down drunks to children. The little brats ate nothing. Where's LouLou?

(HAROLD goes to phone and starts dialing.)

BENJI. Getting dolled up in the bedroom. Candi's helping her. *(Confidentially.)* She's wearing a dress with slits.

HAROLD. And you let her wear it?

BENJI. I'm her accompanist, not her priest.

HAROLD. *(Into phone.)* Bernice? ... *(Resentfully.)* I'm at LouLou's ... Well, you should've told me you wanted the ice cream ... *(Aside, to BENJI.)* That woman needs ice cream like I need hair spray. *(Back into phone.)* ... The paper plates? How many? ... We'll keep 'em. Sooner or later there's bound to be another birthday for a kid named Stevie ... I'll call you later.

(Hangs up and sits down on sofa. BENJI joins him. They share some of HAROLD's party food.)

BENJI. Wait till you see Lou. She's acting like a school girl. This could set her off again.

THE INCOMPARABLE LOULOU 45

HAROLD. Especially after last night's fiasco. *(Shrugs.)* I don't understand that man. He's married.

BENJI. This may come to you as a shock, but politicians cheat too.

HAROLD. Did she say where they're having dinner?

BENJI. Why? You want to cater it? *(Sound of Buzzer.)* That's him...

(CANDI enters and quickly crosses to front door.)

CANDI. When did they fix the intercom? *(She goes to the intercom on the wall near the front door and presses the button.)* Yes? Hello? *(There is no response. Into intercom again:)* Hello? Hello? *(She presses the button several times.)* They put in the intercom, but they forgot to connect it. *(She crosses to window. HAROLD and BENJI quickly follow her. As CANDI opens window, impressed.)* A limo!

HAROLD. Sure. Him they let double park.

CANDI. There he is! Oh, my goodness, he's a good-looking man.

BENJI. That's the chauffeur.

CANDI. Oh. *(She whistles, then shouts.)* Hello there! LouLou will be right down!

LOULOU. *(O.S. Also shouting.)* I need you in here, Candi!

(CANDI quickly goes toward bedroom.)

CANDI. *(Quietly.)* I think she still loves him.

HAROLD. I think you think too much.

CANDI. *(Practically swooning.)* It's like one of her French songs.

*(CANDI exits to bedroom.
Sound of Doorbell.)*

HAROLD. How the hell did he make it up so fast?

CANDI. *(O.S. Calling:)* Can somebody get the door?

(BENJI, exasperated, goes to door and opens it. Standing there in U.S. Congressman JACK LATHAM. JACK is a handsome man, several years younger than LOULOU. Overly friendly. Obviously a good politician. He's wearing an expensive suit and is holding a single red rose in one hand, a gift package in the other.)

JACK. Benji! What a nice surprise.

HAROLD. *(Reaching for the rose wrapped in cellophane.)* I'll take that.

JACK. Why, thank you, Harold. Harold Bains, right?

HAROLD. *(To BENJI, mock appreciation.)* He remembered.

JACK. Of course I remember. We go all the way back to LouLou's first Ed Sullivan Show. *(To BENJI.)* He used to bring her coffee from next door.

BENJI. Harold's a caterer now.

JACK. Is that so?

HAROLD. *(Hands him a card.)* Yeah. I specialize in political affairs. I once catered a first communion for Geraldine Ferraro's niece in Queens. *(Proudly.)* A hundred and one cacciatores.

BENJI. Wasn't that a Walt Disney movie?

JACK. You've come a long way from that little greasy spoon you used to own.

BENJI. So, what are you up to these days, Jack?

JACK. You're kidding, right?

BENJI. Managing any big stars?

JACK. I've been a U.S. Congressman from Arizona for the last five years.

HAROLD. *(To BENJI.)* How come we didn't hear about that here?

BENJI. We've got to start reading the *National Enquirer.*

JACK. Shouldn't someone tell LouLou I'm here?

BENJI. *(To HAROLD.)* Why don't you tell her?

HAROLD. Why don't *you*?

JACK. Why don't I tell her? *(Calls out.)* LouLou!

(CANDI comes running out of bedroom.)

THE INCOMPARABLE LOULOU

CANDI. She'll be right ... *(Sees JACK, is obviously impressed with his looks.)* You're LouLou's ex?

JACK. *(To CANDI.)* And you're ... ?

CANDI. *(Extending her hand.)* I'm LouLou's friend from downstairs. Candi, with an "i" ... *(She shakes his hand.)* So, this is what a Senator looks like.

JACK. *(Correcting her.)* Congressman.

BENJI. The father-in-law's the Senator.

CANDI. Oh, that's right. You're married.

HAROLD. They're all married, politicians. It's good for their image.

(As JACK turns to deposit the gift package on piano, LOULOU appears at the bedroom door. Her basic black dress, now with medium-high slits, suddenly looks quite stylish. We recognize several colorful CANDI "touches," camouflaging part of the dress. JACK turns around. He stares at LOULOU. She stares at him. The others in the room look from LOULOU to JACK, back to LOULOU, then to each other. Within the first few seconds, we get a sense of what LOULOU and JACK must have meant to one another at one time.)

JACK. Lou, you look sensational.

LOULOU. And you don't look so bad yourself. *(An awkward beat.)* You remember Benji and Harold, of course.

JACK. Of course. We were just ... reminiscing.

LOULOU. And you met Candi. *(JACK nods and smiles.)* We do volunteer work together.

CANDI. We spent the other night at the Maritime Union around the corner. We served soup to old sailors with no teeth.

JACK. How charming.

LOULOU. I put a drop of sherry in it. They are very happy. They all smile like this. *(Demonstrates—smiles, covering her teeth with her lips. They laugh. LOULOU continues, not knowing what to say.)* Can I offer you a drink?

BENJI. *(Jumps in.)* Great idea.

(He heads for bar.)

HAROLD. *(Party tray in hand.)* Why don't I defrost some grape leaves or some little egg rolls? It'll only take thirty, forty minutes.

LOULOU. Never mind, Harold.

HAROLD. *(To JACK—offering tray.)* Unless you happen to be a peanut butter and jelly man. I got those ready to go.

JACK. Thank you, but we have a dinner reservation.

(HAROLD produces JACK's red rose.)

HAROLD. *(To LOULOU.)* Here, he brought you *one* flower.

LOULOU. *(Takes the rose.)* Thank you, Jack. I love roses.

HAROLD. This isn't "roses." *(Holds up one finger.)* This is "rose."

CANDI. It's beautiful.

(BENJI returns with three drinks already poured.)

BENJI. *(Handing one each to LOULOU and JACK.)* Here you go. *(To JACK.)* You like bourbon, don't you? Sure you do. All politicians like bourbon.

HAROLD. Of course they do.

BENJI. *(Raising his glass.)* Well, here's to the sovereign state of Alabama.

(BENJI drinks.)

JACK. Arizona.

HAROLD. *(Who has also gotten a drink.)* To Alabama!

(LOULOU, who continues to stare at JACK, addresses her friends.)

LOULOU. Harold, don't you have to get back to Bernice?

THE INCOMPARABLE LOULOU 49

HAROLD. No, it's all right. She can wait. There's no rush.

LOULOU. And Benji, don't you have to go home and try some new wonderful dessert?

BENJI. Are you kidding? If I eat anymore, I'll bust.

LOULOU *(To CANDI, who is standing next to her.)* And Candi, you don't want to keep your boyfriend waiting, do you?

CANDI. He's not home yet. *(LOULOU gives her an obvious shove.)* Well, I suppose I could walk my dog.

LOULOU. All right, everybody, 'bye-'bye!

(Waving to all of them as they slowly drift OUT.)

JACK. Nice seeing all of you.
HAROLD. *(To LOULOU.)* Call me if you need me.

(HAROLD exits.)

BENJI. (To LOULOU.) I'll check with you later.

(BENJI exits.)

CANDI. *(To JACK.)* Any friend of LouLou's is a friend of mine.
JACK. Thank you.

(CANDI exits, closing door behind her.)

LOULOU. They mean well. They like to protect me.
JACK. Oh? Do you need protection?
LOULOU. *(Anxious to change the subject.)* Do you really want that bourbon, or should I get you some wine instead?
JACK. *(Nods.)* Wine would be nicer.

(JACK goes to put his glass on the écritoire.)

LOULOU. *(Calls out.)* Jack! My antique.

JACK. *(Quickly lifting his glass away.)* Sorry. *(Looks at écritoire, smiles.)* This was the first thing we ever bought together.

LOULOU. *(As she crosses to kitchen area.)* We bought it, *I* paid for it.

JACK. Touché. *(He stops in front of one of LOULOU's large posters on the wall.)* The good old days.

(LOULOU unwraps Jack's rose, puts it in a vase and gets a bottle of wine.)

LOULOU. I know it looks a little egotistical, but my friends like them, so I put them up.

JACK. No, they're terrific. They always were. *(He notices the gigantic stove in the kitchen.)* I see you've taken up cooking in a big way.

LOULOU. *(Laughs.)* That stove is from Harold's first restaurant. He says it will come in handy for all the parties I'm always giving.

(She begins uncorking the wine bottle.)

JACK. I noticed Benji and Harold still hate me.

LOULOU. I don't think they ever forgave you for leaving me.

JACK. *(Coming towards her. After a beat:)* And you?

LOULOU. *(Handing him the bottle—anxious to change the subject.)* Here. The least you can do is open the bottle. *(She crosses to sofa with the wine glasses and the rose on a tray.)* Your wife is well?

JACK. Very well, thank you.

LOULOU. Is she still as amusing as ever?

JACK. *(Opens bottle.)* You haven't changed, have you?

(He joins her at the sofa, pours two glasses of wine.)

LOULOU. I think it was in *Cosmopolitan* I read where she had a job nose?

THE INCOMPARABLE LOULOU

JACK. *(Laughs.)* Jennifer's very honest that way. She didn't feel she had anything to hide.

(He sits next to her.)

LOULOU. Well, it was not easy to hide such a nose.
JACK. *(Reprimandingly.)* LouLou. (He hands her a glass of wine.) What should we toast?
LOULOU. To your career in Washington.
JACK. And to many more successes like you had last night.
LOULOU. *(Turning away from him.)* I don't know how many more I can take like that.
JACK. *(Savors the taste of the wine; closes his eyes—with authority.)* The Loire Valley.
LOULOU. Non, the Napa Valley.
JACK. God, I almost forgot what you friend Yvette sent you from Paris.

(He quickly goes to package he placed on piano.)

LOULOU. Was your wife with you in Paris?
JACK. No, I was alone. *(Hands her gift.)* Here.

(LOULOU opens package, finds card. She reaches for her eye glasses, thinks better of it. She holds card away from her. Finally holds it at arm's length and begins to read it as JACK smiles.)

LOULOU. "Ma chérie, I think of you all the time. I miss you very much. Love, Yvette. *(She removes item from wrapping. It's a 12-inch Eiffel Tower souvenir replica. LOULOU is genuinely moved.)* Ah, la tour Eiffel. It's beautiful. This makes me feel happpy.

(LOULOU gets up and takes it to écritoire.)

JACK. Are you happy these days.?

LOULOU. Yes. Surprised?

(She places Eiffel Tower on écritoire.)

JACK. Is there someone in your life?
LOULOU. Well, I see a few people. But basically, I have put the automobile in the garage.
JACK. *(Laughing.)* Isn't that a bit premature?
LOULOU. *(Matter-of-factly.)* I can always take it out again.
JACK. *(Smiles.)* Whatever happened to that producer you were seeing?
LOULOU. Oh, that one. Very nice man but no "prestidigitation."
JACK. *(Smiles.)* Most people would settle for the word "magic".
LOULOU. You are the one who used to teach me new words. Did you forget? "Five new words every week ..."
LOULOU and JACK. "... improves the English that we speak."

(They both laugh.)

JACK. And you were a very good pupil, too.

(LOULOU starts searching through drawers of the écritoire.)

LOULOU. Except with the "t-h". It took me a whole year to go from "zis" to "*th*is". From "zat" to "*th*at". From "zoes" to "*th*ose". I even had trouble telling people I was Mrs. Jack La*th*am.
JACK. Well, maybe your next husband will have an easier name.
LOULOU. I am not looking for a husband, Jack.
JACK. But you have so much to give.
LOULOU. Give, give. You know, people who give, sometimes also like to receive. Here, I found it.

(She retrieves a school notebook and leafs through it.)

THE INCOMPARABLE LOULOU 53

JACK. Is that the same book? Here, give it to me, I'll test you. *(He takes book, flips pages, reads random words.)* Pristine.
LOULOU. Unspoiled. Untouched.
JACK. Very good. Palpable.
LOULOU. *(A beat.)* Can be touched.
JACK. Another word for cautious.
LOULOU. Oh, I know that one. Circum ...
JACK. *(Edging her on.)* That's it, circum ...
LOULOU. Don't help me. *(Snaps fingers.)* Circumspect.
JACK. That's it. *(They laugh. He puts notebook down, reaches for her hand, tenderly, and slowly pulls her down on sofa next to him.)* LouLou, you are some terrific lady.
LOULOU. *(Finding the moment awkward.)* What time did you make the reservation?
JACK. Oh, we have time.

(He gets up, goes to record player.)

LOULOU. By the way, where are we eating?
JACK. I thought we'd go to the Russian Tea Room.
LOULOU. Ooh, I love blinis and caviar.
JACK. Remember that Russian place we used to go to in Paris?

(He finds one of LOULOU's record albums.)

LOULOU. Of course. Chez les Russes.
JACK. That's the one.

(He starts removing record from album jacket.)

LOULOU. What are you doing?
JACK. *(Shows her album with her picture on it.)* Don't you want to hear my favorite singer?
LOULOU. Do we have to? *(Phone rings. LOULOU quickly answers it as JACK puts record on record player. She speaks softly.)*

Allo ... ? No, I'm fine, Benji ... Everything is fine ... We're leaving now ... The Russian Tea Room. 'Bye.

(She hangs up. One of LOULOU's pretty ballads, "I'd Love To Fall Asleep", starts to play.)

JACK. You know, I called Benji a few years ago.
LOULOU. *(Surprised.)* He never told me.
JACK. He hung up on me.
LOULOU. Good for him. *(A beat.)* Why were you calling him?
JACK. To find out about you. *(LOULOU looks at him.)* I was interested. *(A beat.)* I've missed you. *(He goes to her, extends hand.)* Dance?
LOULOU. But are you crazy?
JACK. *(Innocently.)* I just want to dance.
LOULOU. Jack, really.

(JACK gently pulls her up and leads her to area behind the sofa, and they begin to dance.)

JACK. You know, you're looking exceptionally well.
LOULOU. Thank you. So are you.
JACK. I try to keep in shape. I work out at the gym, three, four times a week.
LOULOU. Me, I do yogurt.
JACK. *(Laughs.)* I think you mean "yoga." *(She nods, as they keep dancing.)* Do you still remember the words?
LOULOU. Of course. Two things you never forget in life. Songs and lovers.
JACK. Would you sing for me?
LOULOU. Jack, this is really silly.
JACK. *(Imploringly.)* Please.

(LOULOU begins to sing as they glide across the floor, recreating steps they used to share.)

THE INCOMPARABLE LOULOU

LOULOU.
I KNEW YOU'D COME ALONG ... TO MAKE MY LIFE A SONG
JUST LIKE AN ANGEL FROM ABOVE
I'D LOVE TO FALL ASLEEP
AND WAKE UP IN YOUR ...

(She breaks away.)

LOULOU. (Cont.) This is foolish.

(JACK goes to her, holds her again, as they resume dancing.)

JACK. Are you still wearing that same perfume I used to get you?

(He gently strokes the top of her back with one hand.)

LOULOU. No. "Folie de Nuit" used to give me a headache. This is a free sample from Bloomingdales. Jack, your hand.
JACK. Which one?
LOULOU. The one that is working overtime.
JACK. What about it?
LOULOU. Tell it to stay still.
JACK. Oh, it won't listen to me. I never did. *(As he moves his hand around her waist, he suddenly lets out a scream.)* OWW!

(They stop dancing.)

LOULOU. That will teach you to go around feeling ex-wives.
JACK. *(Imploringly.)* LouLou ...
LOULOU. *(Imitating his exact tone.)* Jacques ...
JACK. You know what you just called me?
LOULOU. No, what?
JACK. Jacques. You only called me Jacques when we made love.
LOULOU. *(Mockingly.)* Oh, are we making love now? I could not tell.

(LOULOU sits on sofa. JACK gets the bottle of wine and goes to sofa.)

JACK. More wine?
LOULOU. No, thank you. I'm saving a little room for my blinis.
JACK. You know, I was thinking, LouLou. Would you mind very much if we stayed in and spent the evening here? Just the two of us.
LOULOU. What about the Russian Tea Room?
JACK. To tell you the truth, I had a huge lunch today. I really would prefer something lighter.
LOULOU. But everything I have is frozen, except maybe for some cheese poofs.
JACK. *(Imitating her.)* I *love* cheese poofs.

(He goes to phone and dials.)

LOULOU. Good-bye, caviar.
JACK. We've got so much to talk about.
LOULOU. We do?
JACK. *(Into phone.)* Oh, hi! Congressman Latham here. Something's just come up. I'll have to cancel my table. Thank you. *(Hangs up.)* This evening is having a very strange effect on me—and it's not the wine, either. I feels if time didn't exist, as if we'd never separated.

(He joins her on the sofa.)

LOULOU. Well, control yourself. It does exist, and we're very much separated. It's called divorced.
JACK. I think this mens something to you, too.

(He moves closer to her.)

LOULOU. Are you crazy or what?
JACK. *(Teasingly.)* What?

THE INCOMPARABLE LOULOU

LOULOU. What's your problem?

JACK. I'm affectionate. You should know that better than anyone.

LOULOU. You know, you're being a little ridiculous playing the part of seducer.

JACK. Oh, yeah? Well, the "seducer" is about to kiss you.

(He moves closer to LOULOU.)

LOULOU. Are you not ashamed of yourself?
JACK. You can't tell me this isn't nice.
LOULOU. Nice, but ...
JACK. But what?
LOULOU. *(Softening.)* Well ... I suppose one kiss is not going to matter all that much.

JACK. Exactly. After all, we're not kids. We've been through so much together. The good times, the bad times. The ups, the downs. We've known wonderful moments and not so wonderful moments.

LOULOU. *(Interrupting.)* This kiss—is it coming or what?

(JACK kisses her. It begins as a warm, tender kiss. It slowly progresses to something more passionate.)

JACK. It all comes back, doesn't it?
LOULOU. Like riding a bicycle.

(They kiss again. This time he puts his arms around her tightly and immediately lets out another scream and jumps away.)

JACK. OW!!! I'm bleeding. What's going on here?

(LOULOU hands him a paper napkin for his finger and gets up, laughs.)

LOULOU. Well, you see, my dress was ... *(She's about to indicate that is was too tight but decides to indicate that it was too large instead.)* My dress was much too big on me, so Candi helped me pin it.

JACK. Only you would do such a thing. *(Indicates finger.)* I'd better go run some cold water on this. Can I use your washroom?

(JACK gets up.)

LOULOU. *(Indicates bedroom door.)* Just go through there and follow my posters. My career leads right to the bathroom. *(JACK exits as she goes to écritoire and addresses it.)* Listen, you've been around for a few hundred years—what's going on here? *(Phone rings. She answers it.)* Allo? ... No, everything is fine, Harold. We're on our way out now ... The Russian Tea Room.

(JACK re-enters, now without jacket. He starts toward LOULOU.)

LOULOU. *(Cont.) (On phone, as she hangs up.)* Good idea, Harold. We'll try the Shashlik ... Thank you. 'Bye.

(JACK approaches her. He takes the phone off the hook, then goes to embrace her but hesitates-wary of the pins. He takes her face in his hands and kisses her as the
Curtain Falls.)

END OF ACT I

ACT II

Scene 1

(The next morning.
HAROLD is on the phone. The apartment is like it was when we last saw it.)

HAROLD. *(Into phone.)* Well, I'm sorry I ran out of the house so early this morning, Bernice. I had things to do ... Are you sure that's tonight? A sit-down dinner for two hundred people ... all sushi. Well, at least we won't have to cook. *(He laughs meekly. Sound of Doorbell.)* I gotta go. Start slicing.

(Hangs up, goes to door, opens it. It's BENJI.)

BENJI. What are you doing here?
HAROLD. *(As BENJI enters.)* I could ask the same thing.
BENJI. Yeah, well, I beat you to it. Where is she?
HAROLD. She's not here.
BENJI. She's never been up this early in her life, let alone out of the house.
HAROLD. Her phone was busy all night. I stopped calling around three. Bernice was furious.
BENJI. The line wasn't busy. It was off the hook. I had the operator check.
HAROLD. I think she's gone.
BENJI. Of course she's gone if she's not here.
HAROLD. No, I mean "gone" ... with ... *him.*

BENJI. How can you be sure?
HAROLD. It's pretty obvious. Wait here.

(HAROLD quickly goes to bedroom as BENJI walks around looking for clues. He goes to stereo, picks up record albums. Starts reading titles.)

BENJI. "If I Love," "Love Me Now", "Come Get Your Love", "Love Me Quick ..."

(HAROLD returns with empty wine bottle and two empty glasses.)

HAROLD. What do you call these?
BENJI. *(Nods knowingly.)* They were probably playing ... *(Indicates record.) these* before they went to bed with... *(Indicates wine and glasses) those.*
HAROLD. *(Noticing scattered photos on écritoire.)* What do you make of these?
BENJI. *(Comes over to him.)* Photos. They must have been reminiscing.
HAROLD. That's the one thing LouLou shouldn't be doing.
BENJI. (He suddenly notices Eiffel Tower on écritoire.) What's this?
HAROLD. I think it's the Eiffel Tower.
BENJI. I *know* that. I mean what is it doing here? I've never seen that here before.
HAROLD. *(Picks up the note.)* I'll bet this goes with it.
BENJI. Let me see that. *(Takes it from him, starts reading.)* "Ma chérie, I think of you all the time. I miss you very much ... Love ..." *(Shows note.)* What does that say?
HAROLD. I think it says Jack.
BENJI, Of course it says Jack.
HAROLD. But it's not clear.
BENJI. That's 'cause he's too cagey to make his signature legible. Where do you think he took her?

THE INCOMPARABLE LOULOU 61

HAROLD. *(Giving it a lot of thought.)* Let's see. Where would I take her?

BENJI. I'm not interested in where you would take her. I want to know where that 'politician' took her.

HAROLD. *(Handing BENJI the single rose from last night.)* What about this? Does that give us anything?

BENJI. That's yesterday's flower. *(Throws rose aside.)* How can that possibly help us?

HAROLD. I don't know. I'm new at this.

BENJI. If she's fallen for him again, we're *all* in trouble. I don't know if LouLou can handle any more rejection.

(Sound of keys in the door. BENJI and HAROLD freeze. In enters LOULOU, carrying a large dress box.)

LOULOU. *(Surprised to see them.)* What are you two doing here?

(They both go to her.)

BENJI. Your phone wasn't working all last night.

HAROLD. And this morning when we called, nobody answered. So we were concerned.

BENJI. Yeah, we were worried.

LOULOU. I think it's time you stopped treating me like a child. I also think you should give me my keys back, Harold.

HAROLD. But you said I should have a set in case of an emergency

LOULOU. *(Indicates dress box.)* You call this an emergency?

BENJI. *(Suspiciously.)* Can we ask you what's in the box?

LOULOU. What is the matter with you two? I went out and bought a suit.

HAROLD. *(Suspiciously.)* Somebody treat you?

LOULOU. No, I treat myself. I guess you could say I will be wearing my antique clock.

(LOULOU starts for bedroom.)

HAROLD. *(Relieved.)* Benji thought you were running away with Jack.

BENJI. What do you mean, Benji thought? We both thought.

LOULOU. *(Laughing.)* Run away with Jack? Are you completely insane? Why would I run away with Jack? He's married. And he went back to Washington.

(LOULOU exits to bedroom humming the song she and JACK danced to the night before.)

BENJI. Aha! Did you hear that singing? That's the singing of someone in love.

HAROLD. But she just said there was nothing going on.

BENJI. Do you think she knows what she's saying? I'm telling you, that conniving Congressman got to her.

(Sound of Doorbell. HAROLD goes to door, opens it. CANDI, holding bouquet of roses, comes in.)

CANDI. These just came for LouLou. *(LOULOU re-enters from bedroom.)* I took them from the delivery boy. I hope you don't mind. *(Hands her the card.)* Here, read the message. It's real cute. *(LOULOU takes the note and reads it as CANDI goes to the kitchen and puts roses into a vase.)* I counted them. Eleven roses.

HAROLD. What's the matter with that guy? Why can't he ever put together a dozen roses?

LOULOU. Benji, it's such a beautiful day, let's rehearse.

BENJI. For what?

LOULOU. Just for the fun of it. *(She leads him to piano.)* Let's do "I'd Love To Fall Asleep." But not like we did it on the record, a little brighter.

HAROLD. *(As he sits and gets comfortable.)* My favorite.

THE INCOMPARABLE LOULOU

(LOULOU sings "I'd Love To Fall Asleep"—part of it in French. While singing, the Doorbell Rings. It's loud and persistent. HAROLD goes to answer it.)

LOULOU. *(Stopping HAROLD.)* That's my sister. Let her wait.

(LOULOU finishes the song, with CANDI joining her for the last few bars in harmony. Sound of persistent Doorbell. CANDI opens door. BARBARA Enters, holding two shopping bags from New York's finest stores.)

BARBARA. A morning musicale? *(As she comes to sofa.)* By the way, there's a bum sleeping in your hallway downstairs.
LOULOU. Think of him as an eccentric doorman.

(BENJI, HAROLD, and CANDI laugh.)

BARBARA. *(Looking at all of them.)* Well, it's a small audience, but it's loyal.
BENJI. *(Starting towards door.)* I just remembered a previous rehearsal with "someone or other."
LOULOU. No, stay, Benji.
HAROLD. *(Also moving toward door.)* And I probably have something to cater "somewhere or other."
LOULOU. Don't go, Harold.
CANDI. *(Innocently.)* I'm not busy.
BARBARA. *(To LOULOU.)* I picked up the contract for your memoirs.

(BARBARA takes out contract from bag. BENJI and HAROLD stop, look at one another.)

CANDI. *(Impressed.)* You have memoirs?
BENJI. When did you write your memoirs?

LOULOU. It's nothing. I just wrote down a lot of silly things that I remembered.

HAROLD. Are we in there?

LOULOU. Of course you're in there. *Everybody's* in there. It's my life, my work, my friends ...

BARBARA. And her salvation.

HAROLD. Gee, imagine that. Me in a book.

BENJI. How come we didn't know about this? We know everything else.

LOULOU. *(Exchanging kisses with them at the door anxious to change the subject.)* You know, I was thinking of making a nice homemade lunch for us tomorrow. Are you free?

HAROLD. *(Quickly.)* We'd love to. What time?

BENJI. *(Suspiciously.)* You don't cook.

LOULOU. Late morning—noonish.

BENJI. Come, Candi, let's leave the Brontës alone.

CANDI. *(Daydreaming.)* God, I wish *I* had memoirs.

(CANDI and HAROLD exit.)

BENJI. *(Without missing a beat.)* You will!

(He exits.)

BARBARA. *(Dialing phone.)* My lawyer went over the entire contract. Just sign on the last page.

LOULOU. *(Starts looking at contract.)* As soon as I read the fine print.

BARBARA. It's all fine print. *(Referring to phone call she's making.)* Damn answering machine. *(Into phone, as she tries on newly purchased shoes.)* When you get back to your desk, Kim, would you tell my husband that I saw the most perfect piece of real estate this morning. *(Aside.)* If it weren't for me, he'd be just another doctor. *(Into phone.)* And Kim, tell him I'm on my way to Bergdorf's to have my hair done. After which I have some things to pick up at

Bendel's, which means I can probably meet him for a late lunch at La Granouie around two o'clock.

(BARBARA hangs up.)

LOULOU. Ahhh, it's a full life.
BARBARA. *(She gets up; excitedly clutching some of the books.)* Do you have any idea where this could all lead to? We're talking mini series, features, cassettes. By the time I get through, Edith Piaf will be paté next to you. *(Hands LOULOU a pen.)* Here, sign.

(Sound of Phone Ringing. BARBARA, who is closer, picks it up and answers.)

BARBARA. (Cont.) Hello ... Who is this? .. Jack? ... Jack who? ... *(Shocked.)* Jack Latham?!!! ... *(Looks over at LOULOU and sits down. Flattered.)* Barbara ... Barbara Milner. LouLou's sister ... I haven't been Barbara Walsh for years ... You remember when I was Barbara Dorn? ... What a memory! ... Yes, she's here ... Nice talking to you, too. *(Cups phone and hands it to LOULOU.)* Why is *he* calling *you*?
LOULOU. *(Flippantly.)* Ex-husbands, they do that sometimes.
BARBARA. Mine don't.

(BARBARA watches LOULOU suspiciously.)

LOULOU. Allo?... Jacques? ... Yes, I feel wonderful. And you? ... How are things in Washington? ... You're still *here*? ... You mean *now*? ... But, Jacques ... Jacques? ... *(Hangs up.)* You better leave. He's down the street. He called from his limo.
BARBARA. What is going on here?
LOULOU. Nothing is going on.
BARBARA. Louise! You're thinking of cooking. Something is going on.
LOULOU. *(After a beat. Being blasé about it.)* I saw him last night.

BARBARA. *(Her eyes widen.)* You *saw him* and you didn't tell *me*? Oh, my God. What did he say? What did *you* say? What did he *want*?

LOULOU. Nothing. He was just passing through town and, uh...

BARBARA. *(A sudden thought.)* You know, I heard he might be up for a big cabinet post. *(She stops in front of the "mirrored wall" and puts on fresh lipstick.)* Wouldn't it be something if he got it? Our book would go through the roof. *(A beat.)* Why is he coming back anyway?

LOULOU. He's coming back because, uhh ... *(Going to Eiffel Tower on écritoire and picking it up.)* Did I show you what he brought me?

BARBARA. *(Studies statue for a beat.)* What a sport!

(LOULOU puts it back carefully.)

BARBARA. *(Cont.)* Wait a minute. You're not stupid enough to start up with this opportunist who single-handedly ruined your career.

LOULOU. You seem to forget he was the one who brought me to America.

BARBARA. He did you some favor. You were a big star in France. Now, look at you.

LOULOU. *(Defensively.)* Jack was a very good manager for me. He took care of everything.

BARBARA. *Everybody* always took care of *everything* for you. It's about time you took control of your own life, and do what I tell you. Sign the goddamn contract.

(BARBARA shoves contract in LOULOU's hand.)

LOULOU. He will be arriving any minute.

BARBARA. Believe me, I'm out of here. *(She quickly gathers her things.)* You know what I'd do when he gets here? I'd pump him.

LOULOU. Pump him?

BARBARA. Get more material for the book. Oh, this is exciting.

THE INCOMPARABLE LOULOU 67

I'm gonna need a whole new wardrobe. You, too. We're going to do all the talk shows—The Tonight Show, The Today Show, the works. *People* magazine will want to photograph you. You'll use my place, of course.

LOULOU. Jack knows not to use the elevator.

BARBARA. *(A sudden thought.)* After you get rid of him, why don't you join me and Harvey for lunch at La Granoie?

LOULOU. No, thank you. I have to look nice and slim for the book jacket. By the way, it's pronounced "La Grenouille."

(LOULOU pronounces it "Grenooye")

BARBARA. Yes, well, while you're here pronouncing it, I'll be there eating it. I'll be back for the signed contract tomorrow morning—eleven-thirty *sharp. (Her hand on the door knob.)* Sometimes it's almost worth having been married to them just to have the pleasure of getting even.

(BARBARA opens the door. Standing there is JACK LATHAM.)

JACK. *(To BARBARA.)* You're not ... My goodness, I never would have recognized you. You look at least ten years younger than when I last saw you. It is Barbara, isn't it?

BARBARA. *(Flattered.)* Jack, please.

JACK. My congratulations to the doctor.

BARBARA. How did you know he was a doctor?

JACK. Aren't they all?

LOULOU. Except for the pharmacist. Of course, she was very young then. *(BARBARA gives her a dirty look.)* Au revoir.

BARBARA. Let's not forget the "pump."

JACK. *(Turning to LOULOU.)* Something wrong with your plumbing?

BARBARA. *(Smiling happily.)* Her plumbing is fine. Everything is fine. In fact, I can't remember when things were any finer.

JACK. I've never seen you this happy.

BARBARA. Really? You should see me shopping.

(BARBARA exits. LOULOU and JACK move about with a certain awkwardness.)

LOULOU. Thank you for the lovely roses, Jack. Can I offer you some wine?

JACK. Oh, no, it's much too early for wine. Coffee, if you have it.

LOULOU. I hope you are in the mood for a lot of coffee. Harold gave me a coffeemaker that can only make forty cups.

(LOULOU goes to kitchen area. JACK smiles, walks around.)

JACK. I haven't laughed as much as I did last night in a long, long time.

LOULOU. Me, neither.

(LOULOU returns with small sandwiches on a tray.)

JACK. I had a wonderful time. And I think you did, too.

LOULOU. Look, I had a moment of weakness, but I have completely recovered. (As JACK makes a move towards her, she shoves the platter of sandwiches in front of him.) Here, have a sandwich.

(JACK takes a small sandwich, starts eating it.)

JACK. I've missed you over the years, Lou. I can't tell you how many times I wished I could come back to see you and talk to you, or just sit and say nothing. *(Reacts to sandwich.)* Did I just eat a peanut butter and jelly sandwich?

LOULOU. *(Laughs.)* Sorry. Everything else is frozen stiff. I'll get the coffee.

(LOULOU gets up. So does JACK. He walks over to écritoire.)

JACK. I always loved this piece. It's so "you."

LOULOU. *(From kitchen area.)* Now you are comparing me to an old piece of furniture.

JACK. You know what I mean. It's beautiful. It's classic. It has style. *(Picks up and looks through some loose photos.)* Hey, what are these?

LOULOU. *(As she returns with coffee and cups.)* Just a bunch of old photographs. I was looking at them this morning after you left.

JACK. I love old photos.

LOULOU. There's more inside—in my shoe box.

(JACK opens écritoire, takes out shoe box with rubber band around it.)

JACK. Must be valuable stuff.

LOULOU. Like you always used to say, I am not the best organized person in the world.

(JACK takes shoe box to sofa.)

JACK. *(Indicating rubber band.)* May I?

LOULOU. If you still remember the combination *(JACK removes rubber band and cover with mock flair. He sits and places the box on his lap and looks at photos.)* I thought you had to be back in Washington today.

JACK. I won't tell if you don't. *(Picks up photo.)* Is that Benji with you?

LOULOU. *(Looks at photo.)* Look how skinny he was before he met George.

JACK. *(Another photo.)* Oh, my God, is this the hotel in St. Paul de Vence?

LOULOU. Our first weekend.

JACK. That was the most beautiful day I had ever seen.

LOULOU. It was raining.

JACK. *(Lost in thought.)* I know.

LOULOU. If you look real close, you can see me slipping you money under the table.

JACK. I don't remember that. *(He picks up another photo.)* Look at this. We really looked like two people in love, didn't we?

LOULOU. I thought we were.

JACK. *(Suddenly concerned as he looks at another photo.)* What's this?

LOULOU. Backstage in Las Vegas, after my show. You, me, and the Martoni brothers. I think that was Guido.

JACK. Are you crazy, leaving pictures like this around?

(JACK gets up.)

LOULOU. I don't leave them around. They are in a safe box with a rubber band.

(LOULOU takes the photo back from JACK.)

JACK. But the Martoni brothers ...

LOULOU. They were your friends.

JACK. *(Defensively.)* They were my *clients*. I did their P.R. work, that's all. Believe me, I've never seen them since.

LOULOU. I'm not surprised, since one of them was murdered and the other one is in prison for life.

JACK. Yeah, in prison but now operating one of the biggest drug rings in the country.

LOULOU. How do you know all this?

JACK. Don't you read the papers? The man has been in the news for months. These aren't the kind of pictures you're planning to publish, are you?

(There is a long awkward pause as LOULOU reacts to his knowledge of her memoirs.)

THE INCOMPARABLE LOULOU

LOULOU. *(Hurt and angry.)* No wonder I hear from you after all these years.

JACK. *(Walks away.)* What are you talking about?

LOULOU. I'm curious, Jack. How did you find out about my memoirs?

JACK. What memoirs?

LOULOU. *(Meaning "I'm not a fool".)* Jack!

JACK. Okay, I happen to know someone at Doubleday. He tipped me off.

LOULOU. Well, you sure did a nice job. Between the dancing and the romancing and your show-stopping performance last night. *(Applauds.)* Bravo! As an old trouper, I always appreciate a good spectacle.

JACK. *(Going to her.)* Lou, I admit, when I came here yesterday, my intentions were somewhat less than above board.

LOULOU. Above board?

JACK. But the minute I saw you, I realized just how much you meant to me and I couldn't bring myself to talk about your book. You have to believe that.

LOULOU. I believe what I see. And what I see ... *(She stares at him.)* I still don't believe.

JACK. Lou, I found myself a niche in politics. I like it. I'm good at it. I think I can make a difference.

LOULOU. *(Walks away again.)* And for that, you want me not to have existed?

JACK. I never said that.

LOULOU. I remember when your "niche" was managing me.

JACK. People grow.

LOULOU. You had a very good deal with me, Jack.

JACK. Really? Do you think it was such a picnic being known as Mister LouLou?

LOULOU. *(Amused.)* Is that what they called you?

JACK. Among other things.

LOULOU. So why did you not speak up?

JACK. There was no time, remember? You were working, always working.

LOULOU. *(As she crosses down to piano.)* So that's what it was.

JACK. It wasn't "one" thing. It was ... *(Anxious to get back on track.)* Lou, I may be up for a big cabinet post. I even met with the President last week.

LOULOU. And you think the President will be embarrassed because twenty years ago we went half-naked in the fountain at Rockefeller Center.

JACK. I don't remember that.

LOULOU. I forgot it, too. One more for my book.

JACK. I don't suppose I could talk you into letting me have that photo.

I'll do even better than that.

(She tears photo into pieces.)

JACK. Thank you.

LOULOU. I have the negative.

JACK. You know, a picture of me with the Martoni brothers ... Well, the truth is, it could taint my reputation. Damn it. Lou, this isn't France where scandals are a way of life. *(He goes to her.)* Your book is ill-timed. The Senate loves to grill people like me. I don't think you understand.

LOULOU. I understand perfectly well, Jack. While I was on stage singing all those years, you were out making all kinds of important connections, including the one with the senator's daughter. And me, like an idiot, I introduced you to her.

JACK. Jennifer Caldwell was not the cause of our breakup, Lou. She was the *result* of it. You know damn well. I never even went near another woman while we were together.

LOULOU. Sure, you were no fool. You were waiting for the jackpot.

JACK. You very conveniently forgot that I spent every single moment I had taking care of your career.

THE INCOMPARABLE LOULOU 73

LOULOU. Oh? P.R. work for the Martoni brothers, was that taking care of my career?

JACK. I was trying to build us a nest egg ... for the future. Just because you never thought about our future, doesn't mean I didn't.

LOULOU. Well, your future worked out very nicely. And now it's my turn. *(Holds out shoe box with photos.)* My future will be in publishing my past. Interesting, non?

JACK. I'm not here to stop you for publishing your book. I wouldn't even dare ask you.

LOULOU. Then what do you want, Jack?

JACK. Maybe we can work out some sort of financial arrangement.

LOULOU. I keep forgetting that you work in Washington. It's a bribe, right?

JACK. It's not a bribe. I have a simple business proposition. Nothing more, nothing less. *(LOULOU stares at him.)* Publish your book, as is, but give me the right to edit those sections that involve me. And for that ... *(Reaches into his jacket.)* I will give you ... *(Takes out an envelope.)* ... this check, already signed, dated, and made out to you.

LOULOU. *(Quietly devastated.)* Where was this check last night?

JACK. In my pocket.

LOULOU. *(Looks at him for a long moment.)* I don't want your money.

JACK. Why can't you be practical for once in your life?

LOULOU. I am trying very hard to remain calm. If nothing else, my therapy teach me that.

JACK. Lou, I need an answer by tomorrow morning.

LOULOU. Please take your check.

JACK. No, you keep it. It's yours, no matter what you decide. *(He puts the envelope on écritoire.)* Think of it as alimony I never paid you. *(He makes his way to door and stops.)* I beg you to at least think about my proposition.

LOULOU. And I impel you to stop being so unctuous. I am not about to be dissuaded. I promise I will not vilify you. Have you noticed how loquacious I have become? There you have it. *(Holds up five fingers.)* My five new words for today.

JACK. You've gotten tough, Lou.

LOULOU. *(Quickly.)* I live in New York.

JACK. We had something very special once, you and me. That's not going to go away, whether it's in a book or not. *(He comes Downstage to her.)* I never meant to hurt you, Lou. Never.

LOULOU. *(Trying very hard not to crumble.)* As they say in Paree ... C'est la vie!

JACK. *(Goes to hold her.)* Lou ...

LOULOU. *(Moves away.)* You don't want to miss the 11:45 elevator.

(JACK returns to door, opens it.)

JACK. *(A beat.)* Au revoir.

LOULOU. *(Her back to him.)* No, au revoir suggest we might see each other again. I think your word is better this time: *good-bye,* Jacques.

JACK. *(Tenderly.)* Good-bye, LouLou.

(JACK Exits. She pauses, then turns and heads toward the écritoire, touches it lovingly. She sits on steps, next to it, and addresses it.)

LOULOU. It's time we started thinking about going home, you and me ... No, I mean it this time. I could drive you out to Versailles to see your old house. *(Forces a smile.)* Maybe you could meet a nice armoire and settle down. And I could give you some free advice, like, never marry someone you love so much.

*(She bursts into tears.
Lights Fade.)*

Scene 2

(The next day.
PETER DESMOND, the antique dealer, is examining the écritoire, which he has pulled away from the wall. He calls out to LOULOU.)

PETER. You certainly kept it in good condition.
LOULOU. (O.S.) Thank you, Peter. It's a remarkable piece of furniture, non?
PETER. Yes ... uh ... Remarkable.
LOULOU. (O.S.) Take your time.
PETER. I am.
LOULOU. (O.S.) It's been with me for many years.
PETER. It must be difficult for you to part with.
LOULOU. (O.S.) It is.
PETER. You're sure you don't want to reconsider?
LOULOU. (O.S.) Non. I've made up my mind.
PETER. What made you decide now, after all this time?

(LOULOU enters, wearing a new, tasteful suit. She's holding a cloth cover for the écritoire.)

LOULOU. I have decided to go "high-tech". To match my mirror wall. I found its cover. So, how much is it worth?
PETER. You look very attractive. That's a beautiful suit.
LOULOU. Merci.
PETER. Is it a special occasion?
LOULOU. I'm taking my friends out to lunch to celebrate the sale of my écritoire. So, how much is it worth?
PETER. Well ...
LOULOU. *(Pressing.)* Well?

(PETER looks at LOULOU, walks around the écritoire once more.)

PETER. Well ...
LOULOU. I think it's my turn again. Well?
PERTER. It's a little difficult to say.
LOULOU. Let me help you. Is it in the neighborhood of eighty, ninety thousand dollar?
PETER. Try another neighborhood.
LOULOU. *(Resigned.)* Okay. sixty. *(PETER just stares at her. A little apprehensively:)* Fifty? *(PETER continues to stare at her.)* Forty? *(A beat.)* Thirty? Don't tell me twenty.
PETER. I won't tell you twenty, because it's not even ten.
LOULOU. *(Incredulous.)* What?!!!
PETER. I dreaded the day you'd ask me about this. I never thought you'd have to sell it.
LOULOU. You knew all along that it was worth less than ten thousand dollar?
PETER. It's not even worth five.
LOULOU. *(Astonished.)* A Louis the Sixteen écritoire, all the way from France? And you tell me it's not even worth five thousand dollar?
PETER. I'm not sure it's worth more than a few thousand.

(LOULOU is visibly shaken.)

LOULOU. Don't tell me it's a postiche.
PETER. *(Takes a deep breath.)* Worse. It's a phony.
LOULOU. That's what postiche means. But how can that be? I bought it in the Faubourg St. Honoré. It was at the peak of my career. I can still remember the man who sold it to me. He told me it would be an investment for life.
PETER. I don't know what to tell you.
LOULOU. Tell me it's not true. Tell me I did not spend all these years talking to a fake.

(PETER looks at her curiously.)

PETER. Maybe there's some sort of recourse, if you still have a receipt.
LOULOU. Do I look like a woman with receipts?
PETER. I feel terrible.
LOULOU. Why should you feel terrible? All you did was make a French woman cry today.

(She sits down on sofa.)

PETER. *(Looking at her posters on the walls.)* I have a client who collects old posters. If you'd like, I'll put you in touch.
LOULOU. *(Lost in thought.)* What did you say?
PETER. I said, some of your posters may be worth something.
LOULOU. No, no. I am not interested. There is a limit to how much of yourself you can sell.
PETER. I'm sorry.
LOULOU. It's not your fault.
PETER. *(Heading for door.)* I have to be at an auction by noon. It's not a bad copy. I'd keep it if I were you. *(He looks over the apartment.)* It, uh ... it does something for the apartment. Good-bye.

(PETER Exits, closes the door. She slowly looks over at the éritoire, her anger building. She gets up and goes towards it.)

LOULOU. You rotten liar. You no-good thief. How could you? How could you do this to me?

(She picks up cover and starts hitting the écritoire with it.)

LOULOU. (Cont.) And I thought you were my friend. All these years, moving you from place to place, costing me money, never knowing where to put you ... Teaching people how to pronounce your name. I am furious at you! Menteur! Trompeur! Vaus rien! Salaud!

(Throws cover at it. She then picks up two of the books BARBARA left behind.)

LOULOU. (Cont.) You leave me no choice. If I have to publish, I publish. Too bad for Jack. *(She throws book at it.)* Too bad for me. *(She gets ready to throw second book—Sound of doorbell.)* Saved by the bell, you bastard. *(Throws book down. Doorbell again.)* Coming!

(She goes to door, opens it. CANDI is standing there with her small dog in her arms.)

CANDI. *(Agitated.)* Listen, I need a very big favor from you. My girlfriend is in big trouble. I may have to go spend the night with her, and she's allergic to dogs. So I was wondering if you might be able to take care of Theodore just for tonight.

(CANDI gives dog to LOULOU.)

LOULOU. *(Trying not even to look at the cute dog.)* Gee, I really don't know anything about animals.
CANDI. *(Holding back tears.)* I knew you'd understand. My girlfriend will be forever grateful.
LOULOU. What's wrong, Candi?

(LOULOU goes to put dog on the floor.)

CANDI. *(Shouts.)* Don't! *(LOULOU quickly holds the dog up.)* I haven't walked him yet. Maybe you should put him in the bathroom.
LOULOU. Good idea. Don't move. I will be right back. Have some coffee. *(She starts to go. She looks at the dog and addresses it.)* You are very cute, you know that, Theodore? Naturally, you *would* have a name with a "T-H".

(She Exits to bedroom.

THE INCOMPARABLE LOULOU

As soon as LOULOU has left the stage, CANDI runs out of the apartment and closes the door. LOULOU returns.)

LOULOU. (Cont.) So, what exactly is going on with ... *(Looks around.)* Candi? Candi? Candi, where are you?

(LOULOU rushes to door, opens it, and runs out. Several moments later, LOULOU returns, carrying a large piece of luggage and dragging CANDI in. CANDI is holding a stuffed Teddy Bear.)

LOULOU. *(Cont., as she sits CANDI down on sofa.)* Now, come in here and tell LouLou *everything*. Talk nice and slowly. Remember, English is not my mother tongue. First of all, where are you going?
CANDI. I'm going home to Thunder Hawk. I'm catching a Trailways bus at Port Authority at three.
LOULOU. You're going to *Th*under Hawk? At Port Au*th*ority at *th*ree? Are you just saying these words to aggravate me?
CANDI. Life sucks!
LOULOU. Not even twenty years of age and you have the nerve to say that life sucks? What do you know about life?
CANDI. So what's so wonderful about it?
LOULOU. I'll tell you what's so wonderful about life. *(A beat.)* Your question is stupide. *(She sits on arm of sofa.)* So your trumpet player ran away with someone else.
CANDI. He didn't so much run away as she moved in.
LOULOU. Non.
CANDI. Oui.

(CANDI starts crying again.)

LOULOU. And for that you are running away to *Th*und ... *Th*und ... to that place? *(Gets up, goes to front door.)* Once you get to New York, you don't leave so fast. You stay here and you fight. *(Closes front door and returns to CANDI.)* Show me your hand. *(Takes*

CANDI's hand, examines it.) Just what I thought.

CANDI. What?

LOULOU. Things are looking up for you. You are going to go from the *first* floor to ... the *fifth* floor.

CANDI. I can't do that.

LOULOU. Why not? The *th*ree of us on the fif*th* floor. You, me, and *Th*eodore. It will be a T-H festival. Imagine, a beautiful girl like you getting depressed over some boy when there are so many in this world.

CANDI. How could he do this to me? Especially the day before my audition.

LOULOU. You have an audition tomorrow and you are going back to the Dakotas today? Now I *know* you are from the Dakotas.

(She places CANDI's head on her lap, and during the following, because of the passion in her voice, she accentuates her words by inadvertently pounding CANDI's head.)

LOULOU. (Cont.) I'll tell you what's so wonderful about life. Friends. Good friends. When you have good friends, little moments of joy somehow keep coming along. Then, before you know it, something really big happens, like an audition ... or a man. Let's face it, we can all use one from time to time. In order for people to be at their very best, they need a broken heart now and then. What we have to do is learn how to use it. How to use it in life. How to use it in our work. Candi, go to the piano.

(CANDI gets up, a little shaken by the experience.)

LOULOU. (Cont.) You know, I only heard you sing a few times. And to tell you the truth, I wasn't listening very closely. Sing something.

(CANDI gets her music from her luggage and goes to piano as LOULOU goes with her.)

THE INCOMPARABLE LOULOU

CANDI. I wrote some new lyrics last night ... while she was unpacking in the other room.
LOULOU. Let's hear them.

(During the following, LOULOU goes to bar, pours herself some red wine, and goes to écritoire where she opens a drawer and takes out the publishing contract. All along, LOULOU reacts to CANDI's new lyrics.)

CANDI.
NOW I'M NO A GEN-IUS, BUT I'M NOT A DOPE
AND I HAVE LEARNED A REAL IM-POR-TANT LES-SON, I HOPE
DON'T WAN-NA BE A MIC-ROBE UNDER YOUR MIC-RO-SCOPE
IF YOU'RE MAD I'M SOR-RY
BUT BABY THAT'S THE STORY
SO FIND ANOTHER GUINEA PIG
FOR YOUR LABORATORY
I'M NO LOVE SPECIMEN
I'M NO LOVE SPECIMEN

(LOULOU places her wine glass on top of écritoire.)

CANDI. *(Cont. Stops playing and singing.)* Your écritoire!
LOULOU. That's the beauty of not owning antiques.

(Sound of Doorbell.)

CANDI. I'll get it.

(CANDI goes to front door, opens it. HAROLD and BENJI Enter.)

HAROLD. Are we too early for lunch.
LOULOU. Lunch has been cancelled.

BENJI. *(To HAROLD.)* You owe me a buck.

LOULOU. *(With contract in hand.)* I have just now made a very important decision. Come. Help me with this. *(They all join her.)* Everybody takes a piece of Doubleday. *(She hands sections of contract to them.)* Now, all together.

(LOULOU tears the pages. They tear the pages.)

HAROLD. What are we doing?
LOULOU. We're preserving my dignity. Rip!

(She shreds her section into little pieces and throws them over her head—they do likewise.)

CANDI. It's just like New Year's.
LOULOU. It's better than New Year's. We are also celebrating my getting a roommate.
HAROLD and BENJI. *(Apprehensively.)* Him?
LOULOU. *(Pointing to CANDI.)* No, her. Oh, my God. I forgot. Nobody move. *(She goes back to écritoire and the others stand in place. She retrieves JACK's envelope, opens it and looks at the check.)* Ooh la la. The Congressman has done very nicely for himself.

(LOULOU shows them the check.)

CANDI. I never saw so many zeroes.
LOULOU. You know what I'm going to do now that I have some financial backing? I'm going to open a small supper club.
HAROLD. *(In awe.)* Your name in lights.
BENJI. What do you know. I'm working again.
LOULOU. It will be a small club for people who don't like loud music. *(To CANDI.)* I will present young talent like you. Of course, you will have to sing softer. *(Sound of Doorbell.)* And, Harold, you will make the food. *(HAROLD opens door. BARBARA enters. LOULOU calls out.)* Right on time.

THE INCOMPARABLE LOULOU 83

BARBARA. Where's the contract?

LOULOU. *(Indicates shredded contract on floor.)* There, there and there. I'm opening a small supper club instead.

BARBARA. *(As she walks over.)* What are you talking about?

LOULOU. *(Waves check at BARBARA.)* If you want your money back, you will have to bring all your rich friends as customers.

(BARBARA looks at check; she is impressed.)

BARBARA. *(Kisses LOULOU.)* Now I know you're my little sister. Where are you planning to open this club?

LOULOU. I don't know yet. This idea is only one minute old.

BARBARA. What about next door?

LOULOU. What do you mean?

BARBARA. *(All smiles.)* I just bought the building.

LOULOU. Fantastique! *(ALL join in the enthusiasm. As she removes her jacket, LOULOU reveals a glittering blouse.)* Of course, as the hostess ... *(She nods to BENJI.)* Benji, s'il vous plais. *(BENJI immediately goes to piano and sits.)* I may be persuaded now and then to get up and sing.

BENJI. Ladies and gentlemen ... The Incomparable LouLou!

(BENJI starts playing as group applauds. The lighting changes in the apartment. LOULOU's posters on the walls are highlighted. The place turns into a small intimate club. As she makes her way to the piano, a lighted chandelier drops over the piano. LOULOU picks up a real microphone nearby. A spotlight hits her and follows as she begins to sing her hit song, "La Vie est Belle".)

LOULOU.
TU TE REVEILLE
UN RAYON DE SOLEIL
ET SOUDAIN
LA VIE EST BELLE

UN OISEAU CHANTE
UNE ROSE T'ENCHANTE
ET VOILA
LA VIE EST BELLE

TU DIT BONJOUR A L'AMOUR
ET L'AMOUR TE DIT BONJOUR

OH, C'EST BEAU LA VIE
QUAND ELLE TE SOURRIS
ET QU-ELLE TE DIT
LA VIE EST BELLE

LOVERS IN FRANCE
WHEN THEY LOSE AT ROMANCE
THEY STILL SHOUT
LA VIE EST BELLE

NOTHING CAN LAST
SO WHY LIVE IN THE PAST
CALL IT OUT
LA VIE EST BELLE

REMEMBER, LIFE IS TO LIVE
COME ON, FORGET AND FORGIVE

JUST OPEN YOUR HEART
GIVE YOUR LIFE A NEW START
WHAT THE HELL
LA VIE EST BELLE.

(As LOULOU continues singing, a blue, lit, neon sign drops. It reads, "Chez LouLou".)

LOULOU. (Cont.)
LA LA LA LA
LA LA LA LA LA LA
LA LA LA
LA VIE EST BELLE

LA LA LA A
LA LA LA LA LA LA
LA LA LA
LA VIE EST BELLE

LA LA LA LA LA LA LA
LA LA LA LA LA LA LA

LA LA LA LA LA
LA LA LA LA LA LA
WHAT THE HELL
SING, LA VIE EST BELLE

(Final Curtain)

END OF PLAY